MW00644049

The People
versus
Jesus

The People versus Jesus

A study of Jesus' claims
to be God

Louis H. Evans, Sr.

WORD BOOKS
PUBLISHER
WACO, TEXAS

THE PEOPLE VERSUS JESUS

Copyright © 1949, 1976, 1980 by Louis H. Evans, Sr.
All rights reserved. No part of this book may be reproduced in any form, except for brief quotations in reviews, without the written permission of the publisher. Purchase of this book does not convey the right to produce the play. Permission to produce on a nonroyalty basis must be obtained by writing Word Books, Waco, Texas 76703.

Library of Congress catalog card number: 79-56173
ISBN 0-8499-2909-1

Printed in the United States of America

Quotations from The Revised Standard Version of the Bible (RSV) copyrighted 1946, 1952, © 1971, 1973 by the Division of Christian Education of the National Council of the Churches of Christ in the United States of America, are used by permission.

Quotations from The New English Bible (NEB) © The Delegates of The Oxford University Press and The Syndics of The Cambridge University Press, 1961, 1970, are reprinted by permission.

Quotations from the New American Standard Bible (NAS) are copyright © 1960, 1962, 1963, 1968, 1971 by The Lockman Foundation.

Quotations from The New Testament in Modern English (Phillips) by J. B. Phillips, published by The Macmillan Company, are © 1958, 1960, 1972 by J. B. Phillips.

Quotations from The Living Bible Paraphrased (LB) published by Tyndale House Publisher, 1971, Wheaton, Ill., are used by permission.

Quotations from The Bible, A New Translation, by James Moffatt, are copyright 1922, 1924, 1926, 1935 by Harper & Bros.

Quotations from The Bible: An American Translation by Edgar J. Goodspeed, J. Powis Smith, et al., are copyright 1923, 1935, 1948 by the University of Chicago.

Quotations marked Weymouth are from The New Testament in Modern Speech by Richard Francis Weymouth, published by The Pilgrim Press, 1943.

Quotations from Today's English Version of the Bible (TEV), © American Bible Society 1966, 1971, 1976, are used by permission.

Contents

Contents

Part Three
CHRISTIANS AND JEWS

Preface

Why This Book?

There are several reasons for this book and this play. The original title under which the play was produced gives the first one: "Who Is This Man?" or "Christ on Trial." Here we have the question that *defines and affects the veracity and person of Jesus Christ* who made unquestioned claims to deity. He himself asked the all-important question, "Who do you say that I am?" He demanded of all who heard him the right verdict.

Mt. 16:15, RSV

A second reason is that *the future of the church* will depend upon our verdict. Jesus asked this question of his disciples who were to establish with him the first Christian churches. Peter, probably as spokesman for the group, answered, "You are the Christ, the Son of the living God." Christ's approval of Peter's answer was immediate and reaffirming: "Blessed are you, Simon Bar-Jona! For flesh and blood [mere human wisdom] has not revealed this to you, but my Father who is in heaven. And I tell you, you are Peter [*petros* in the Greek, meaning a *piece* of rock or a stone, masculine singular], and on this rock [*petra* in the Greek, neuter, a rocky ledge, cliff, a stone quarry, or a rocky substratum]"—out of all who believe that I am the Son of God—"I will build my church, and [if you build it out of such people] the powers of death [gates of hell,

Mt. 16:16–18, RSV

7

KJV] shall not prevail against it." But they must believe this of me (my deity).

The church is built not so much upon Peter or the believer, as upon Christ. The Apostle Paul warns us, "No other foundation can any one lay than that which is laid, which is Jesus Christ." He is the chief "cornerstone" holding the building together. Without him the temple of God crumbles. It is the confession of Christ that makes us Christians, and that makes us grow "into a holy temple in the Lord, in whom you also are built into it for a dwelling place of God in the Spirit." Peter also states in his first epistle that we, "coming . . . to a living stone [Christ], disallowed indeed of men, but chosen of God . . . as lively stones, are built up a spiritual house, an holy priesthood . . . acceptable to God by Jesus Christ . . . and he that believeth on him shall not be confounded."

1 Co. 3:11, RSV

Ep. 2:21–22, RSV

1 Pe. 2:4–6, KJV

Until *we* answer this great question of Christ's firmly and understandably, facing any challenge with certainty, we will remain unsure of the key to every primary spiritual problem which we may encounter: *Prayer*—"If you ask anything of the Father, he will give it to you in my name"; *sin*—"The Son of man has the authority . . . to forgive sins"; *behavior*—"I am the way"; *empty lives*—"I came that they may have life . . . abundantly"; *knowledge of God*—"He who has seen me has seen the Father"; *death*—"He who believes in me . . . shall never die"; *coming to God*—"No one comes to the Father but by me"; *truth*—"I am the way, and the truth, and the life"; *fear*—"It is I; be not afraid"; *obedience*—"If you love me you will keep my commandments"; *fatigue*—"Come to me . . . and I will give you rest."

Jn. 16:23, RSV
Lk. 5:24, RSV
Jn. 14:6, 10:10, RSV
Jn. 14:9, 11:25, RSV
Jn. 14:6, RSV
Mk. 6:50, KJV
Jn. 14:15, RSV
Mt. 11:28, RSV

Third, *our future is determined* by faith in the Son of God. "No one who denies the Son has the Father. He who confesses the Son has the Father also." "Who-

1 Jn. 2:23, RSV; Jn. 3:16, RSV

8

ever believes in him [has] eternal life." Christ said, "Unless you believe that I am He [I AM, in Greek, referring to Exod. 3:14], you shall die in your sins." "Who is the liar but he who denies that Jesus is the Christ?"

Jn. 8:24, NAS
1 Jn. 2:22, RSV

Fourth, answering this question *is necessary to our witness.* Christ commissioned us all to "go into all the world and preach the gospel to every creature." If Christ indwells us he is too big for us to contain—he must overflow us. If he does not overflow us he does not indwell us. We only keep him as we share him; if we do not share him we lose him. After his resurrection Jesus appeared to his disciples and others and said, "You shall receive power when the Holy Spirit has come upon you; and you shall be my witnesses in Jerusalem and in all Judea . . . and to the end of the earth."

Mk. 16:15, RSV

Ac. 1:8, RSV

Why are Christians not better witnesses? There are several reasons.

1. Some just *do not care.* Indifference can blind us to need.

2. Some *are not informed.* One man said to me, "Dr. Evans, I don't know enough about my faith to debate it." One leader said, "The average church member is about as well equipped to stand up to a Wellsian agnostic or a Marxian communist as a boy with a peashooter is to go against a marching army with cannon." A great Christian lawyer of Washington, D.C., said, "The main trouble with the Kingdom of God is tongue-tied laymen!"

3. It is an age of *spiritual bankruptcy.* Since the act of "Separation of Church and State," we have allowed the act to deteriorate into a separation of God from education. We never meant to do that. Many a campus has become an academic spiritual desert with youth starved for God. A university president said, "The average collegian has immense limbs, a medium-sized

9

head, and a very shriveled soul. The task of education is to help the soul catch up with the body and the mind." Taking the letters G, o, and d, out of *good* leaves us with o—nothing to build on. Morality has lost its highest aid—God. But many Christians are seeing some rays of light: concerned action! This is evidenced in innumerable Bible study groups and the sales of religious material.

This drama was written during my Pittsburgh pastorate when we and much of the world were experiencing a prewar spiritual slump which also embraced a failing Christology and creedal cramps.

There are continuous religious revivals because religion keeps "losing" Christ. Dr. James S. Stewart, the Scottish theologian, feels that while we retain the two-thousand-year-old memory, forget Christ's as a "living presence" today. "We have kept Him as an object of our veneration and our worship but we have lost Him as a herald voice to be obeyed. We have kept Him as the school of liberal theologians kept Him, as the greatest leader who ever led the hosts of humanity, the finest teacher that ever taught, the noblest example—but we have last Him as God incarnate in the flesh." [1]

Sensing this uncertainty with their own minds, the students in my church in Pittsburgh suggested we give some three months' study to the deity of Christ, as they desired more evidence for their faith. I suggested that, instead of a long list of bibliographies and literary treatises on human theories penned by various writers, we study the scriptural records of the sayings, acts and works of Christ. Out of this research and study came this drama. The students cast it themselves, and such was the blessing to the actors and the enthusiastic

---

1. James S. Stewart, *The Life and Teachings of Jesus* (Nashville: Abingdon Press, 1958).

reception by the audiences, that other churches began to ask for the script in order to present the drama themselves.

During my Hollywood pastorate, professional Hollywood actors presented the drama, usually four times a Sunday, to accommodate the audiences that thronged the church.

My hope and prayer is that reading this play devotionally, producing it dramatically, or presenting the thrilling sound cassette,[2] may fortify your faith, and further embolden and clarify your witness for Christ.

PRELIMINARY NOTES

In the play, marginal notes give Scripture references, and also refer to Parts Two and Three of this book, indicating the sections where some possible problem or question is researched and dealt with. Some of these items may add to the clarity of your witness and the veracity of what your faith affirms.

We hope that the free and careful use of Parts Two and Three will give you a firmer rationale and a more definite reason for the faith within you.

The scriptural quotations of witnesses in the play are mainly from the King James Version (or the Old English). Several dramatists felt this might lead to a more classic dramatic presentation, as in a Shakespearean play.

However, much of the speech of the attorneys and the judge are in more contemporary language. The

---

2. A dramatic reading of the play, entitled "Christ on Trial," is available on cassette tape. Order Cat. No. 140LL from Educational Products Division, Word, Incorporated, 4800 W. Waco Drive, Waco, TX 76703.

material that follows the play uses several translations and language styles for clarity.

In order that individual parts for the play may be provided as described in the Production Suggestions ("Permission to Produce," pp. 57–59), portions of some pages, or in two instances, complete pages have been left blank. No break in continuity is intended; the action proceeds without interruption from beginning to end.

Part One
THE PLAY

The People versus Jesus

CAST OF CHARACTERS

THE BAILIFF, *calls the trial to attention*
THE JUDGE, *the Honorable Mr. Fairness*
THE ATTORNEY FOR THE PROSECUTION, *Mr. Frank Unbelief*
THE ATTORNEY FOR THE DEFENSE, *Mr. Reasonable Faith*

Witnesses for the Prosecution:
KEEPER OF THE GARDEN
PHARISEE
CAIAPHAS
PONTIUS PILATE
(PRIEST—*optional*)

Witnesses for the Defense:
MARY OF BETHANY
NICODEMUS
WOMAN OF SAMARIA
CENTURION
PAUL
WOMANHOOD
NAPOLEON

Enter Prosecuting Attorney, Defense Attorney, to take their places at their respective tables. Bailiff enters to make his first speech, followed by Judge. The witnesses enter as summoned.

BAILIFF: You will all arise. Hear ye, hear ye. All persons having aught to do with the Honorable Judge Fairness of this said court of conscience shall draw nigh, giving their attention. They shall be heard. God save the Commonwealth and this honorable court. Be seated. The case of Unbelief against Jesus of Nazareth.

JUDGE: Gentlemen, are you ready to present your cases?

PROS. ATTY: Ready.

DEFENSE ATTY: Yes, Your Honor.

JUDGE: It is required by law that the defendant be present during the trial of his case. Jesus of Nazareth is here, though unseen. His promise to his disciples was, Mt. 28:20 "Lo, I am with you alway." As they testify then, they shall testify in his presence. He counseled his followers, saying, "And when they bring you unto . . . magistrates, and powers, take ye no thought how or what thing ye shall answer, or what ye shall say. For the Holy Ghost shall teach you in the same hour what ye Lk. 12:11– 12 ought to say." Thus the defendant, through the Spirit, may in truth converse with his counsel. All those who testify for the prosecution also do the same in his presence. He does not care to testify in his own behalf, save through what his witnesses might say.

Mr. Frank Unbelief, attorney for the prosecution, you may proceed. Do you desire to make an opening statement?

PROS. ATTY: I do, Your Honor.

JUDGE: Proceed.

16

Witness: Keeper of the Garden

PROS. ATTY: Ladies and gentlemen of the jury, it is my intention to prove that Jesus claimed to be the Son of God: that on various and sundry occasions he did make these specific claims; did state with unquestioned clarity these claims, and took unto himself the attributes of God; that in each of these cases, his claims were so unquestionable and their implications so clear, that they tried thrice to stone him for blasphemy. Having proved this, the duty that is yours is clear, because we have a law, and by that law he ought to die, because he made himself the Son of God. He is guilty!   Jn. 19:7

My first witness, please.

BAILIFF: First witness for the prosecution, the Keeper of the Garden.

PROS. ATTY: What is your task, my good man?

K. OF GARDEN: I am the Keeper of the Garden of Gethsemane.

PROS. ATTY: Did you ever see Jesus of Nazareth there?

K. OF GARDEN: Often.   Lk. 21:37

PROS. ATTY: What did he do there?

K. OF GARDEN: Came there with his disciples, sometimes alone, to rest and to pray.   Mt. 26:36

PROS. ATTY: Did you ever overhear him pray?

K. OF GARDEN: I did, but quite by accident, of course.

PROS. ATTY: Of course. What did he say?

DEFENSE ATTY: Your Honor, I object to this question as to what he said on the grounds that what a man says in his prayers has nothing whatever to do with the problem of who he is.

JUDGE: This may have some significance. Objection overruled.

PROS. ATTY: I repeat the question. What did he say in praying?

17

K. OF GARDEN: Well, among other things, he said, "Father glorify thou me with . . . the glory I had with thee before the world was."

Jn. 17:5

PROS. ATTY: He used the words "before the world was"?

K. OF GARDEN: He did.

PROS. ATTY: Were you present at a feast in Jerusalem after which some persons had an altercation with Jesus?

Jn. 7:37; 8:12

K. OF GARDEN: I was.

PROS. ATTY: Will you tell us what went on?

K. OF GARDEN: He began by making this statement: "Verily, verily, I say unto you, If a man keep my saying, he shall never see death." Then we replied, "Art thou greater than our father, Abraham, which is dead? And the prophets are dead? Whom makest thou thyself?" And then he replied, "Your father Abraham rejoiced to see my day. And he saw it and was glad." Now, Abraham lived some nineteen hundred years before that day, and knowing Jesus to be a young man, we said to him, "Thou art not yet fifty years old, and hast thou seen Abraham?"

Jn. 8:51–59

PROS. ATTY: And then?

K. OF GARDEN: Then he said this blasphemous thing, "Before Abraham was, I am."

Note 1 F

PROS. ATTY: Was that implication clear?

K. OF GARDEN: It was. He said he lived before Abraham, that he was preexistent.

PROS. ATTY: Then what did you do?

K. OF GARDEN: We tried to stone him again for blasphemy.

PROS. ATTY: Thank you. Your witness.

DEFENSE ATTY: No cross-examination. Thank you.

PROS. ATTY: That's all. Next witness, please.

BAILIFF: The second witness for the prosecution, a Pharisee.

18

PROS. ATTY: Were you at the Feast of Dedication in Jerusalem at which Jesus made some public statements?   Jn. 10:22–39

PHARISEE: I was.

PROS. ATTY: Do you recall seeing Jesus of Nazareth there?

PHARISEE: I do.

PROS. ATTY: Where did you see him?

PHARISEE: He was walking on Solomon's porch in the temple.

PROS. ATTY: Please address your remarks to the jury.

PHARISEE: We crowded around him demanding that he answer some pointed questions. He had made claims that he lived before Abraham, that he was God, and we decided to test finally whether or not he was guilty of those claims and thus of blasphemy.

PROS. ATTY: Did you question him? If so, tell us about it.

PHARISEE: We did question him. We asked him plainly, "How long dost thou make us to doubt? If thou be the Christ, tell us plainly." He replied, "I told you, and ye believed not. I give unto my sheep eternal life."

PROS. ATTY: Did he say anything else?

PHARISEE: He did. He said, "Many good works have I shown you from my Father. For which of these works do ye stone me?" We replied, "For a good work we stone thee not, but for blasphemy, because that thou, being a man, makest thyself God."   Note 1 A,B

PROS. ATTY: Did he deny being God?

PHARISEE: He did not. He said, "If I do not the works of my Father, believe me not." He said his miracles proved that he was God.

PROS. ATTY: And all of this happened at the Feast of Dedication in Jerusalem?

PHARISEE: It did.

PROS. ATTY: Now tell me, were you at the pool of Bethesda near the sheep market at the time Jesus   Jn. 5:1–10

19

healed a man—or claimed to?

PHARISEE: I was.

PROS. ATTY: Can you tell us about that?

PHARISEE: A man was there who had had an infirmity thirty-eight years. Jesus, seeing him lying there, said to him, "Take up thy bed and walk." We said, "It is the Sabbath day; it is not lawful for thee to carry thy bed. There are Sabbath laws in this land," we told him. In defending himself for Sabbath-breaking and making someone else break the Sabbath laws, Jesus made a blasphemous statement.

PROS. ATTY: What was that statement?

Jn. 5:16–18
Note 1 A

PHARISEE: He said God was his Father. In saying this, he used the most intensive pronoun we have— "his very own." We knew then that he was claiming that God had a relationship to him that he had to no man. He was making himself equal with God.

PROS. ATTY: What did you do then?

PHARISEE: We took up stones to slay him.

PROS. ATTY: Thank you. Care to cross-examine the witness?

DEFENSE ATTY: Yes. Now, sir, I doubt not that through centuries, bumptious and arrogant men have claimed to be messiahs, but you say that Jesus of Nazareth said to a man with an infirmity thirty-eight years "Rise and walk"?

PHARISEE: He did.

DEFENSE ATTY: You knew this man to be a cripple?

PHARISEE: I had myself known him for a period of many years.

DEFENSE ATTY: When Jesus said, "Rise and walk," did the man rise and walk?

PHARISEE: Well—uh—uh—

DEFENSE ATTY: I say, did he?

PHARISEE: He did.

DEFENSE ATTY: That is all.

PROS. ATTY: Next witness, please.

BAILIFF: Third witness for the prosecution, Caiaphas, the High Priest.

PROS. ATTY: Will you state your name, please?

CAIAPHAS: I am Caiaphas, High Priest of Jerusalem, member of the Sadducean order, president of the assemblage known as the Sanhedrin.

PROS. ATTY: Was Jesus of Nazareth brought to trial before you?

Note 4

CAIAPHAS: He was.

PROS. ATTY: At what place?

CAIAPHAS: The regular place. The wall of hewn stone in the temple area of Jerusalem.

PROS. ATTY: What was the basis of your questioning?

CAIAPHAS: We questioned him regarding his claims as to his personage. His guilt was established in the mouths of two witnesses.

Mt. 26:57–68

PROS. ATTY: What did they say?

CAIAPHAS: They said that this man said, "I am able to destroy the temple of God and to build it again in three days." Such sacrilege made us all snort with rage. I arose and questioned him further: "Answerest thou nothing?" But he held his peace.

PROS. ATTY: Well, why should he hold his peace? From fear? Had he no answer? From obstinacy? Contempt of court?

CAIAPHAS: Afraid? I think not. Not he.

PROS. ATTY: Contempt of court?

CAIAPHAS: Contempt of everyone. He stood there so utterly sure of himself.

PROS. ATTY: Did he give further speech?

CAIAPHAS: Oh, I forced him to that. I cast this at him: "I adjure thee by the living God, that thou—"

PROS. ATTY: Just a moment, Caiaphas. What's the meaning of that expression, "I adjure thee by the living God"?

CAIAPHAS: That, sir, is the highest form of oath exacted of men who testify. This supreme injunction adjures one, yea, forces, demands that one vary not one jot or tittle from the truth. It is as though man had speech with God Himself. Untruths or even half-truths spoken then perjure a man's soul for all eternity.

PROS. ATTY: What did you ask him under this oath?

Mt. 26:63–68
Lk. 22:67–70
Note 4

CAIAPHAS: I said, "I adjure thee by the living God that thou tell us whether thou be the Christ, the Son of God." Mark you well—"whether thou be the Christ, the Son of God!"

PROS. ATTY: And he said?

CAIAPHAS: He said, "Hereafter shall ye see the Son of man sitting on the right hand of power and coming in the clouds of heaven." I arose and rent my garments in utter indignation of such blasphemy, saying, "He hath spoken blasphemy! What further need have we of witnesses?"

PROS. ATTY: Did you come to a verdict concerning this man?

CAIAPHAS: Turning to my fellows, I said, "What think ye?" And there was not one dissenting voice. They said, "He is worthy of death!"

PROS. ATTY: Did you put him to death?

CAIAPHAS: That is not within our power. Had the nation been independent, the Sanhedrin could have slain him. But since the Roman conquest, our power has been . . . uh . . . somewhat abridged. It was necessary that the Roman government's sanction be obtained.

PROS. ATTY: What did you do then?

Mt. 27:2
Jn. 18:28–32

CAIAPHAS: We decided to take him to the procurator of Judea who alone had the power of the gibbet and the cross. We took him to Pilate.

PROS. ATTY: Thank you. Your witness.

DEFENSE ATTY: It has been asserted, Caiaphas, that

this trial was characterized by certain flagrant illegalities.

CAIAPHAS: That is false, sir!

DEFENSE ATTY: Well, is it not an order of the court that all witnesses for the defense shall be heard first?

CAIAPHAS: Yes.

DEFENSE ATTY: Were any witnesses for the defense of Jesus of Nazareth heard first or last?

Mt. 26:57–68; 27:1–26

CAIAPHAS: None.

DEFENSE ATTY: It is also an order of the court that witnesses for the prosecution shall be warned as to the seriousness of the situation, and that they shall speak from certain knowledge and not from hearsay; were they so warned? (*Pause*) No answer. I think the question is answered. (*Pause*) It is also an order of the court that in cases of serious condemnation and sentence the sentence be delayed for a whole day; but Jesus was condemned on the same day. Is that right?

CAIAPHAS: Yes.

DEFENSE ATTY: Is it not also an order of the court that when these votes are taken, the judges shall rise and hand in their verdicts in writing, the youngest first, individually? But is it not true, Caiaphas, that no sooner had you illegally condemned Jesus of Nazareth than the whole Sanhedrin rose as one angry mob, and according to your own confession, with one voice shouted together, "He is worthy of death"?

CAIAPHAS: Yes, it is true.

DEFENSE ATTY: Now, is it not also an order of the Sanhedrin that in case of serious sentence the Sanhedrin should go into mourning for a whole day and should fast? But is it not true that no sooner had you illegally condemned Jesus of Nazareth than you heaped calumny on his head, blindfolded him, spat upon him? Was there anyone to mourn? Was there anyone to fast?

Note 4

Mt. 26:67

CAIAPHAS: For such as he there were no tears.

23

Cf. Jn.
8:50–52

DEFENSE ATTY: Now, it is said that Nicodemus, one of your number, balked at the whole transaction, claiming that such was the bias that this trial had deteriorated into a mere inquisition.

CAIAPHAS: Nicodemus is hotheaded.

DEFENSE ATTY: But Nicodemus is fair. Is it not true, Caiaphas, that from the very start you tried to make short work of Jesus of Nazareth, tried to trick him into making some statement that would justify you in bringing him before the procurator?

CAIAPHAS: Will you forget his atrocious claims to deity? This . . . this man was procuring an amazing access to the hearts of the people. They reported a raising of Lazarus from the dead in Bethany. We, the rulers, were upset. It would not do for so many to proclaim him to be the Messiah. And should the mobs and the multitudes have marched after him to crown him, the storm of vengeance might have fallen on us by the hands of Caesar, and the Roman legions swept over our land, destroying our temple and with it the last vestige of Jewish nationality. So the assemblage met, knowing that some drastic action must be pursued to quiet this fellow, and that it were better that one man die, than a whole nation perish.

Jn. 11:1–46

Jn. 11:47–52

DEFENSE ATTY: That one innocent man die and thus justice perish with it? By what strange means do some nations strive to live! That is all.

PROS. ATTY: Next witness, please.

(The part of the priest is optional, and may be omitted from the production. For that reason, the dialog with the priest is printed in italics. If this section is omitted, the dialog picks up with the Bailiff's speech calling for Pontius Pilate as the fourth witness for the prosecution.)

24

Witness: Priest

BAILIFF: *Fourth witness for the prosecution, a priest.*

PROS. ATTY: *What is your calling, sir?*

See Part Three

PRIEST: *I am a priest rendering my services under the High Priest of Jerusalem.*

PROS. ATTY: *Were you in attendance at the Feast of Tabernacles in Jerusalem at which Jesus appeared?*

PRIEST: *I was.*

PROS. ATTY: *Will you explain to us the whole procedure and meaning of this feast?*

PRIEST: *It is symbolic in its nature and continues for eight days. On the first day the Chief Priest takes the golden pitcher that is in the temple and carries it down to the Pool of Siloam. There he dips it into the pool and carries it before him, the other priests marching behind him, to the temple where he pours out the water at the golden altar. He does this every day.*

Jn. 7:2, 14

PROS. ATTY: *You said that the feast is of eight days' duration?*

PRIEST: *Yes. The last day is called the Great Day of the Feast. On that day there is one minor but important difference. The high priest does not dip the pitcher into the water but comes back with the empty pitcher carried in front of him—dry. The other priests join with him in the entreaty, "Lord, send us the Messiah!"*

PROS. ATTY: *What does that signify?*

PRIEST: *Many have said that it means that ours is the religion of the empty pitcher; the Messiah for whom we are deeply athirst has not yet come.*

PROS. ATTY: *Did anything unusual happen on the last or great day of the feast?*

PRIEST: *It did. Jesus, seeing us marching back to the temple with the empty pitcher, stepped up and cried: "If any man thirst, let him come unto me and drink. He that believeth in me, as the Scripture hath said, 'From his inmost being shall flow rivers of living water.'"*

Jn. 7:37–39

25

PROS. ATTY: *Was that implication clear?*

PRIEST: *Many believed that he was declaring that belief in him would make it possible for the Spirit to quench the thirst of the soul.*

PROS. ATTY: *Thank you, that is all. Do you wish to cross-examine the witness?*

DEFENSE ATTY: *When Jesus made this declaration—was it done in anger, blasting rebuke, or stern rebuff?*

PRIEST: *No, sir, I would and could not say that. He seemed to declare this in utmost deep, kind concern for our evident emptiness; as though he were challenging us to quench our spiritual thirst by finding in him our fulfilled messianic hope.*

DEFENSE ATTY: *What was the reaction of the priesthood, your fellows, that day?*

PRIEST: *Some were deeply angered and outraged; others of us stared at him in silent awe, secretly wondering if he could in reality be the answer to this insistent thirst for the true Messiah.*

DEFENSE ATTY: *Thank you.*

PROS. ATTY: *Next witness, please.*

BAILIFF: *Fifth witness for the prosecution, Pontius Pilate.*

(If the part of the priest is used, the speech of the Bailiff that follows will be omitted, and the dialog will pick up with the next words of the Prosecuting Attorney.)

BAILIFF: Fourth witness for the prosecution. Pontius Pilate, Procurator of Judea.

26

PROS. ATTY: Your name, please.

PILATE: Pontius Pilate.

PROS. ATTY: In the year A.D. 30, where were you residing?

PILATE: I was procurator of Judea and my headquarters were in the city of Jerusalem.

PROS. ATTY: It was under your jurisdiction, then, that the trial and execution of Jesus of Nazareth took place?

PILATE: Yes. Being a resident of that area, he naturally came under my jurisdiction.

PROS. ATTY: Well, how did he come to you?

Note 5
Lk. 23:1
Jn. 18:28–
30; 19:6–12

PILATE: He had been standing trial at night in the house of Caiaphas, the High Priest. They aroused me in the morning. They did not come into the judgment hall since they were about to eat the Passover and did not wish to be defiled; so I went out to them.

PROS. ATTY: Who brought the charge against him?

PILATE: The Sanhedrin. They wanted my approval on the sentence.

PROS. ATTY: Well, will you tell us what went on?

PILATE: I said to the priests, "What accusation bring ye against this man?" And they answered, "If he were not a malefactor, we would not have brought him up unto thee. He has made himself the Son of God, and we have a law, and by our law he ought to die, because he made himself the Son of God."

PROS. ATTY: Go on, please. Didn't they make other accusations against him?

PILATE: Yes. They said that he had made himself a king and was thus speaking against Caesar. They informed me that he was guilty of treason—plotting to overthrow Caesar.

PROS. ATTY: Proceed.

PILATE: Well, I took him into the judgment hall, and

Jn. 18:33–37   I said to him, "Art thou the King of the Jews?" And he
answered, "Sayest this of thyself or did others tell it
thee of me?" And again I asked him, "Art thou a king

Note 5   then?"

PROS. ATTY: What did he reply?

Note 11   PILATE: He said, "Thou sayest that I am a king. To
this end was I born, and for this purpose came I into
the world."

PROS. ATTY: You condemned Jesus of Nazareth to
death then for two reasons: first, because he claimed
to be the Christ, and second, because he made himself
as a king over Caesar, according to the testimony of the
people.

PILATE: I did. He was executed on the hill, Golgotha,
in accordance with the penal code covering all such
crimes.

PROS. ATTY: Thank you. Your witness.

DEFENSE ATTY: Pontius Pilate, are you thoroughly
satisfied with his sentence handed down concerning
Jesus of Nazareth? Was that honestly your idea of
Roman justice?

PROS. ATTY: Your Honor, I object. This is misleading
and it augurs of crass insult. The record stands.

JUDGE: Please do not give yourself to innuendo. You
have established no ground for your question. Objection sustained.

DEFENSE ATTY: It has been said that as of late you
have peen pacing up and down the halls of your Pala-
tine crying out, "O God, for another chance at Jesus of
Nazareth!"

PROS. ATTY: Your Honor, again I object to this play
upon our emotions. The edict stands; the record has
not been reversed.

JUDGE: Mr. Attorney for the Defense, you will kindly

28

confine yourself to the facts, not to the witness's feelings.

DEFENSE ATTY: After examining this evidence, Pilate, what proclamation did you make to the people?

PILATE: Well, I said to them plainly, "I find no fault in this man."

Jn. 18:38; 19:4, 6

DEFENSE ATTY: No fault in this man! I thought they accused him of making himself a king against Caesar! Is that true?

Note 5

PILATE: No. After investigation I found that when they had wished to crown him king, he pushed the crown away, saying his kingdom was not of this world, else would his servants fight. His spiritual kingdom, he claimed, in no way opposed the temporal kingdom of my emperor, and he told the people also to pay Caesar his proper tribute.

Lk. 20:19–25

DEFENSE ATTY: You discovered then no evidence that he had tried to foment a revolution against Caesar, your emperor?

PILATE: Not to my knowledge, no.

DEFENSE ATTY: I wonder if something else, Pilate, entered into this picture. When the crowd cried, "If thou let this man go, thou art not Caesar's friend," was a fear of the loss of your position something that led you to make this decision?

Jn. 19:12
Note 5

PROS. ATTY: Your Honor, I object to this insinuation. What has this to do with the case?

JUDGE: Perhaps it is relevant. You may answer that question.

PILATE: Well, since Caesar keeps his ear close to the ground, we are warned not to unnecessarily agitate the people. Caesar's domains are widespread. His agents and soldiers are spread thin throughout his conquered domains. We are warned against unduly exciting the people. So when the multitude cried out against him, it was part of political strategy to hear them.

DEFENSE ATTY: Well, would you condemn an innocent man just to quiet a mob?

PILATE: A thousand voices protesting are more than one voice crying out—at least to Caesar and to Rome.

DEFENSE ATTY: Well, what did you do then?

PILATE: Well, realizing I was not on firm ground—what with this whole conflict of my emotions: a message from my wife brought quietly into court warning me not to have anything to do with this just man; the mob outside; the leaders of the people and their accusations; and my respect for this man; the possible loss of my position if I lacked consideration for the political expediencies and pressures of my realm—all these crosslights confused me. So I took up a basin of water and washed my hands of the whole thing and said, "See ye to it."

DEFENSE ATTY: Well, wasn't that your Roman guard placed before the tomb?

PILATE: It was not. Those were not my soldiers, though it was my seal. I said to them, "Ye have a guard. Make it as sure as ye can." It was temple soldiers standing guard there.

DEFENSE ATTY: You've reoriented yourself from this trial for some time. How do you feel about it now, Pilate?

PILATE: "I still remember how I felt disturbed that I must send him to a felon's cross on such a day when spring was in the air and in his life—for he was young to die. How tall and strong he stood, how calm his eyes fronting me straight the while I questioned him. His fearless heart spoke to me through his eyes. Could I have won him to my cause, and a hundred others be-

Note 5

Mt. 27:24–25

Note 9

Mt. 27:62–66

30

sides, my way had led to Caesar's palace, and today I'd wear the imperial purple. But he would not move one little bit from truth. What wants a man with truth when he is young and spring is at the door? He would not listen, and so he had to go. One mad Jew less meant little to the state, and pleasing Annas made my task the less. But for me he spoiled that silver night, remembering he was young and spring was in the air." [1]

DEFENSE ATTY: That is all. That is all, Pilate.

BAILIFF: The next witness.

PROS. ATTY: Your Honor, the prosecution rests.

JUDGE: Mr. Attorney for the Defense, do you wish to make an opening statement?

DEFENSE ATTY: I do, Your Honor.

JUDGE: Proceed.

DEFENSE ATTY: Ladies and gentlemen of the jury, you know the accusation. Jesus of Nazareth is on trial for blasphemy. Now, the prosecution has endeavored to prove to you that Jesus made definite claims to deity, that he claimed that he was the Son of God. This, we, too, affirm; this we do not deny. Now, we do not wish to endeavor to establish the innocence of Jesus on the ground that he did not make such claims. Rather, we wish to establish his innocence by proving that he did have the attributes of God, and this we shall prove through reliable witnesses. If Christ was not the Son of God—

Note 1 A

PROS. ATTY: Your Honor, I object to the name *Christ* as being opinionating.

JUDGE: He is so called by many. Objection overruled.

DEFENSE ATTY: Call my first witness, please.

BAILIFF: First witness for the defense, Mary of Bethany.

---

1. Anonymous

(Play continues without break
at top of page 33)

DEFENSE ATTY: Will you state your name, please?

MARY: Mary.

DEFENSE ATTY: In what town do you reside, Mary?

MARY: In the town of Bethany.

DEFENSE ATTY: Are you personally acquainted with one Jesus of Nazareth?

MARY: I am. He was often in our home. Ever since I was a child, I was taught to look for the Messiah who should deliver Israel. That hope ran like a thread of gold through my young heart. Each night I would pray these words, "I shall see him, but not now. I shall behold him, but not nigh. There shall come a Star out of Jacob, and a Scepter shall rise out of Israel." Often I fell asleep with that prayer upon my lips. Imagine my joy when I discovered Jesus to be the Messiah! *Lk. 10:38–42* *Jn. 11:1–5* *Nu. 24:17*

PROS. ATTY: Your Honor, I object to her conclusions as to who Jesus was. That remains for the jury to decide.

JUDGE: You will confine yourself, Mary, to the facts, not to your faith. Objection sustained.

DEFENSE ATTY: Do you have a sister, Mary?

MARY: Yes. Martha is her name.

DEFENSE ATTY: And do you have a brother also?

MARY: Yes. Lazarus.

DEFENSE ATTY: Did anything unusual happen to your brother Lazarus?

MARY: Yes. Jesus raised him from the dead.

PROS. ATTY: Your Honor, I object. That is only a matter of interpretation. The fact has not been substantiated.

JUDGE: Objection sustained. The claim has not been substantiated.

DEFENSE ATTY: We will substantiate it, Your Honor. Mary, will you relate for us that incident?

MARY: Lazarus, my brother, sick for many days, died. Jesus raised him.

DEFENSE ATTY: Now, not so fast, Mary. Let's go back over the incident a step at a time. Are you sure that your brother Lazarus was dead—that he had not merely swooned or something?

Jn. 11:1–44

MARY: There was no question of that. The physicians declared him dead. He was wrapped tightly in grave-clothes, wound round and round, with a napkin about his head which alone would have suffocated him. So it is our custom to bury, as you know.

DEFENSE ATTY: How long had Lazarus lain in the tomb?

Note 2a

MARY: For four days. Odorous putrefaction proved a state of death.

DEFENSE ATTY: Well, then what happened?

MARY: When Jesus arrived and saw our grief, he asked where we had laid Lazarus. We led him to the tomb. There he wept bitterly, for he loved my brother dearly. And then, in a loud voice, he cried out, "Lazarus, come forth!" And he came forth, hobbling as best as one could in such graveclothes. Then Christ said, "Loose him and let him go." And we unbound him, and he was ours again. Lazarus, our brother, back to life, back to our arms again! That call, "Lazarus, come forth!" shook all Bethany.

DEFENSE ATTY: Did any others witness the raising of your brother Lazarus from the dead?

Note 2b

MARY: Yes. It seemed half of Bethany was at the tomb that day. Many believed on him. How can one doubt a man who can wrestle down death?

DEFENSE ATTY: Do you wish to cross-examine this witness?

PROS. ATTY: No questions.

34

DEFENSE ATTY: Thank you. My next witness, please.
BAILIFF: Second witness for the defense, Nicodemus.
DEFENSE ATTY: Will you state your name, please?
NICODEMUS: Nicodemus.
DEFENSE ATTY: Where do you reside, Nicodemus?
NICODEMUS: Jerusalem, the holy city.
DEFENSE ATTY: What is your position in Jerusalem?
NICODEMUS: I am a Pharisee, a ruler of the Jews. I
am a member of the Sanhedrin.
DEFENSE ATTY: Did you at any time have conversation with one named Jesus of Nazareth?
NICODEMUS: I did. Once I went to him at night to
ask him some questions.
DEFENSE ATTY: Why did you go at night?
NICODEMUS: I was ashamed to let the others know of
my interest in him. They opposed him violently. I did
not care to lose face.
DEFENSE ATTY: Would you kindly relate this conversation to the jury?
NICODEMUS: I started out by saying what every   Jn. 3:1–16
Pharisee deep in his heart could say. I said, "Rabbi, we
know that thou art a teacher come from God, for no
man can do the signs and miracles that thou doest unless God be with him."
DEFENSE ATTY: Well, did he do unusual works?
NICODEMUS: There is no question about that. And
though there was great division amongst us, we all
knew of the good he did. His miracles irked and worried the Sanhedrin greatly. At the council of the chief
priests and Pharisees, they cried out to Caiaphas, the
High Priest, "What do we with this man Jesus, for he   Jn. 11:47
doeth great miracles? If we let him alone, all men will
believe forever on him."
DEFENSE ATTY: There is no question in your own

mind, then, that even your own fellows admitted that he did miracles?

NICODEMUS: That is unquestionable. It is one reason why they feared him so. I saw blind men receive their sight. The lame walked. The dead were raised to live again. The halt ran. And the lepers were made clean.

Note 1 F

DEFENSE ATTY: Your decision, then, as to who Jesus was, was based upon the works that he wrought and the miracles that he did, which were beyond contradiction.

NICODEMUS: Yes.

DEFENSE ATTY: Do you wish to examine this witness?

PROS. ATTY: Nicodemus, are you educated?

NICODEMUS: Yes. In the temple school. As I said before, I am a member of the Sanhedrin. I am instructed in all the law of my fathers.

PROS. ATTY: Couldn't you have been easily prejudiced in favor of Jesus being the Christ?

NICODEMUS: No. For no greater claim can be made by man other than he be the Messiah. There would be nothing harder for me to believe with my background. I do believe.

PROS. ATTY: That's all, thank you.

(Play continues without break
at top of page 37)

DEFENSE ATTY: Call my next witness, please.

BAILIFF: Third witness for the defense, Woman of Samaria.

DEFENSE ATTY: Will you state your residence, please?

WOMAN OF SAMARIA: Sychar of Samaria.

DEFENSE ATTY: Are you married?

WOMAN OF SAMARIA: I have been married five times.

DEFENSE ATTY: Were you at the well of Jacob at the time Jesus of Nazareth visited it?

WOMAN OF SAMARIA: Yes. I met him there one day, and I cannot forget.

DEFENSE ATTY: Will you mind relating to this crowd your conversation with Jesus?

WOMAN OF SAMARIA: He had asked for a drink, and I was loath to give it to him, for the Jews and Samaritans seldom asked favors of each other or received them. When I hesitated, he said, "If thou knewest who it is that saith to thee, 'Give me to drink,' thou wouldst have asked of him and he would have given thee living water." Then he said a strange thing—that if I would drink the eternal water he could give, I would never thirst again. He said very plainly, "I that speak to thee am the Messiah." I knew he was the Messiah.

PROS. ATTY: Your Honor, I object to what she replied. Her conclusion is not founded.

JUDGE: The witness will kindly confine her answers to what happened.

DEFENSE ATTY: Well, what else did he say?

WOMAN OF SAMARIA: He told me to go and call my husband.

DEFENSE ATTY: And what did you say?

WOMAN OF SAMARIA: I told him I had no husband, that I was not married.

DEFENSE ATTY: What did he say?

Jn. 4:4–39

Note 1 D

WOMAN OF SAMARIA: He said, "Thou hast well said, 'I have no husband'—for thou hast had five husbands, and he whom thou now hast is not thy husband. In that saidst thou truly."

DEFENSE ATTY: And what did you say?

WOMAN OF SAMARIA: Well, I knew then that he was a prophet and I told him so. I ran to the village and told the villagers, "Come, see a man which told me all things that ever I did. Is not this the Christ?" We all went out to see him.

DEFENSE ATTY: You would cross-examine this witness?

PROS. ATTY: Did you know Jesus before this meeting?

WOMAN OF SAMARIA: No, I had never seen him before.

PROS. ATTY: Is there any possible way he could have known that you had had five husbands?

WOMAN OF SAMARIA: None whatever. We were total strangers.

PROS. ATTY: Oh. He might have guessed it by accident.

WOMAN OF SAMARIA: I don't believe in accidents like that!

PROS. ATTY: That's all, thank you.

DEFENSE ATTY: Next witness, please.

(Play continues without break
at top of page 39)

BAILIFF: Fourth witness for the defense, Longinus Francinus, the centurion.

DEFENSE ATTY: Will you state your name, please?

CENTURION: Longinus Francinus.

DEFENSE ATTY: What is your calling?

CENTURION: I'm a centurion in the Roman guard, under the rule of Pilate, procurator of Judea, in the service of Caesar, sovereign of the world.

DEFENSE ATTY: Would you mind explaining your duties as a centurion?

CENTURION: It is my task to preside at the executions of all those who suffer death by doom of the gibbet and the cross; for all crimes and treasons punishable by death.

DEFENSE ATTY: You have seen a good many men die then.

CENTURION: I have. Too many.

DEFENSE ATTY: Were you present at the crucifixion of one Jesus of Nazareth on Golgotha?

CENTURION: Yes. I was. It was my task to see that the sentence of death was carried out.

DEFENSE ATTY: Did you notice anything unusual about this man when he died?

CENTURION: Yes, I did. His conduct on the cross impressed me—his spirit, I mean.

DEFENSE ATTY: Well, what do you mean? What did he do? What did he say?

CENTURION: Well, most men dying by crucifixion spit on their persecutors, hurl curses at the crowd. He only said, "Father forgive them. They know not what they do."

DEFENSE ATTY: Anything else?

CENTURION: Yes. His attitude toward the potions offered to him. There were three drinks offered to him

Mk. 15:23,
36
Mt. 27:34,
48
Lk. 23:36;
Jn. 19:29–30
Note 6

on the cross that day, you know. The first was sort of a mock-coronation wine, the drink of kings about to be crowned. This, of course, was offered in ridicule, and he refused it. The second drink was a drug prepared by the women of Jerusalem for men in the throes of crucifixion, to deaden the pain and bring on a merciful stupor. He refused that, too, as if he wanted to suffer the pain to the utmost. Well, the third drink was vinegar, and that was used to wet the parched lips of the sufferer so that he could make a confession before he died. This he took, and moistening his lips with it, he cried out with a loud voice, "Finished!" And then he bowed his head and gave up the ghost.

Note 8

DEFENSE ATTY: Well, there was no confession then of wrongdoing whatever?

CENTURION: Well, it was the absence of any confession of wrongdoing and the loud voice that impressed me.

DEFENSE ATTY: Why did the loud voice impress you?

CENTURION: Because men dying the death of crucifixion usually grow weaker and weaker on the cross. Their last words are little more than dying gasps. He cried out with a loud voice and said, "Father, into thy hands I commend my spirit." And he had only been on the cross about four hours. Now men usually don't die for twenty-four, sometimes even forty-eight hours— that's the lingering agony of crucifixion. But this man cried out with a loud voice and then died. It seemed as if he died just when he wanted to die. I have never seen anything like it.

Note 10
Lk. 23:46

DEFENSE ATTY: Well, what did you do then?

Mk. 15:39
Note 10

CENTURION: Well, I thought to myself, "Truly this was the Son of God."

PROS. ATTY: Your Honor, I object to what he thought as being irrelevant.

CENTURION: Well, I did think it!

JUDGE: The witness will kindly confine himself to the facts. Objection sustained.

DEFENSE ATTY: Do you wish to examine this one?

PROS. ATTY: Longinus Francinus, couldn't you have been a little sentimental that day, just slightly soft in your line of duty? Couldn't your heart have run away with your head?

CENTURION: You are asking that question, sir, of a man whose heart has been hardened by the deaths of more men than you can count your years. I'm a centurion armed with a sword, not sentiment.

PROS. ATTY: Yes, but how are you sure he was dead after those short four hours? He might have merely swooned.   Note 7

CENTURION: We made sure he was dead because of those short four hours. My soldiers pierced his side with a spear, and out of it came blood and water. No man could outlive that thrust. He was dead, and I'll never forget how he died.

PROS. ATTY: That is all.

DEFENSE ATTY: Next witness, please.

BAILIFF: Fifth witness for the defense, Saul of Tarsus.

(Play continues without break
at top of page 43)

41

(Play continues without break
at top of page 43)

Witness: Paul

DEFENSE ATTY: Will you state your name, please, to the jury.

PAUL: Saul, originally; now Paul. Changed for a reason.

DEFENSE ATTY: And your place of residence, please?

PAUL: Once Tarsus and Cilicia, now of the world.

DEFENSE ATTY: What is your vocation, Paul?

PAUL: I am a tentmaker by trade. I studied with Gamaliel, went to the temple school at Jerusalem, then I became an officer for the Sanhedrin, and it was my business to bring Christians in captive and sometimes put them into prison. *Ac. 18:3; 22:3–5*

DEFENSE ATTY: Are you still in that employ? *Ac. 8:1–3; 9:1–19*

PAUL: No, sir. I gave that up because of an experience. I am now serving the church which once I persecuted.

DEFENSE ATTY: Would you mind telling the jury what happened?

PAUL: I had always felt Christ to be an impostor. I felt that he was a blasphemer because he made himself the Son of God. It riled my blood. Therefore, I was glad of the commission to gather his followers together, hunt them down, and put them into prison. I would wipe out this blasphemous sect that made a god of a man. I was on this errand of retribution on my way to Damascus when suddenly a bright light shone from the heavens. It blinded me. I fell to the ground. A voice said, "Saul, Saul. Why persecutest thou me?" I replied, "Who art thou?" He said, "I am Jesus whom thou persecutest." At that moment I realized that this man, Jesus, had been the Christ, the Son of God, and that when I smote the church, I smote him. That was my call. None can gainsay that. Christ appeared to me and now I am worshiping the One whom once I hated.

43

DEFENSE ATTY: Are there any other experiences with him that you could relate?

PAUL: Just this general statement. Christ changed my life. It used to be that the things I would do, I did not. The things I would not do, those I did. Often I cried, "Who shall deliver me from the body of this death?" Christ delivered me. And because Christ lives in me, I am more than a conqueror through him who loved me. The story is too long to tell you now, but what he did in my life only a God could do! Only he could change me from Saul of Tarsus, murderer of Christians, to Paul. He can do this for any man, for any generation.

Ro. 7:14–25

Ro. 8:37

PROS. ATTY: Your Honor, I object to this preaching.

PAUL: I can only speak the things I know and have experienced. Is there any evidence, Your Honor, in this or any other court greater than the evidence of experience? I can say "Once I was, but now I am!" I could, if I were permitted, bring before this court thousands of bodies that have been healed and bound up by his touch, thousands of minds that he has given peace and steadied in all their processes. I can bring thousands of souls that he raised from vileness, sin, habit, and wrong, that now have received the power of his resurrection. This courtroom would not hold them, and when this court has passed away, millions more will follow him.

Cf. Ga. 1:11–24; 2:19–20

PROS. ATTY: Your Honor, again I object. This is neither a pulpit nor a synagogue.

JUDGE: Objection sustained.

PAUL: I only speak the things I know. This man becomes a part of one.

DEFENSE ATTY: Do you wish to cross-examine?

PROS. ATTY: Your Honor, I ask that this testimony be stricken from the record as being merely a personal experience.

44

JUDGE: Personal experience is recognized as acceptable data in the court of experience. Objection overruled. The testimony will stand.

DEFENSE ATTY: Your Honor, since you have ruled that personal experience is acceptable data in the court of experience, I now wish to call to the stand other witnesses of later centuries whose personal testimonies may bear upon the question of who Jesus is.

BAILIFF: Next witness for the defense. Womanhood.

DEFENSE ATTY: Will you state your name, please?

WOMANHOOD: Woman.

DEFENSE ATTY: And where do you reside?

WOMANHOOD: Wherever women dwell and have heard of him.

DEFENSE ATTY: By him, do you mean Jesus of Nazareth?

WOMANHOOD: Yes.

DEFENSE ATTY: Do you know him?

WOMANHOOD: I do.

DEFENSE ATTY: Do you know of any evidence that could rightly be brought before this court that would help us to answer this question that is before us as to who he is?

WOMANHOOD: I believe I have.

DEFENSE ATTY: Would you relate it to the jury, please.

WOMANHOOD: It is the desire of womanhood to judge all religions by what they do for womanhood. No founder of any faith under this whole sun has so sensed our needs as has this Galilean. No one has ever so understood our longings or known what hopes were needed to keep us strong. No one has ever so understood the fetters that bound or the fears from which we would be set free. Wherever he has gone, woman's fetters go. Before Christ appeared, we were nothing but bond

45

servants or chattel. But when he came into the world the mother-heart of Mary sheltered this child, and through her protecting care, he grew to manhood, that he might fulfill his purpose in the world; and through the ages since, because of his mother, men glorified motherhood. And in the days of his flesh he grew to enjoy the companionship of women as revealed in Mary and Martha of Bethany, so that today every woman may claim friendship with him. Before Christ appeared, men considered women to possess no mind. Yet Christ entrusted some of his most profound truths to her keeping, and in the light of those truths given us, I proclaim as woman that he is the Christ, the Son of the living God. With him there is neither male nor female, but all are one in worth. Through all the ages since then, his followers have gone into every land to loosen the bonds that have fettered womanhood and childhood. His messengers went into India and snatched young widows from the funeral pyres. They released girls from the harems of misery and erected schools for them. He himself has set us free. There's little for us in lands where he has not gone. The dignity we have, the freedom we now own, the love with which we are loved, and the blessings we enjoy have come from his hand. No one else could have done this for us. He is woman's Messiah.

Ga. 3:28

DEFENSE ATTY: Do you wish to cross-examine this witness?

PROS. ATTY: No questions.

DEFENSE ATTY: Next witness, please.

BAILIFF: Seventh witness for the defense, Napoleon Bonaparte.

DEFENSE ATTY: The testimony now to be given consists of the words spoken by Napoleon during his exile on St. Helena regarding his changed attitude toward Jesus of Nazareth.[1]

What is your name, please?

NAPOLEON: Napoleon Bonaparte of France.

DEFENSE ATTY: And your title, sir?

NAPOLEON: Emperor of France, ruler of the empire.

DEFENSE ATTY: Did you at any time during your exile have conversation with one named Montholon concerning the personality of Jesus of Nazarus?

NAPOLEON: I did.

DEFENSE ATTY: Would you relate to the jury what went on, what was said?

NAPOLEON: I asked Montholon this question: "Montholon, can you tell me who Jesus of Nazareth was?" He declined the question. Then I answered it for myself. I said, "Alexander, Charlemagne, Caesar, and I founded great empires. But upon what did these creations of our genius depend? Upon force. Jesus alone founded his empire upon love, and to this day millions would die for him. I think I know something of human nature, and I tell you all these were men. I am a man. No one else is like him. Jesus is more than a man. Across the chasm of eighteen hundred years, Jesus makes a demand which is above all others, difficult to satisfy. He asks for that which a philosopher may often seek at the hands of his friends—a father of his children—a bride of her spouse. He asks for the human

---

1. From the writings of Charles Tristan Montholon who accompanied Napoleon to St. Helena. To Montholon, Napoleon dictated notes on his career which Montholon published in books and letters in the early 1800s. (*The Encyclopaedia Brittannica*, 1942, vol. 15).

heart; He will have it to himself entirely. He demands it unconditionally, and forthwith his demand is granted. Wonderful! In defiance of time and space, the soul of man with all its powers becomes annexed to the empire of Christ. All who sincerely believe in him experience a remarkable and supernatural love towards him. The phenomenon is unaccountable. It is beyond the scope of man's creative powers. Time, the great destroyer, is powerless to extinguish its sacred flame. Time can neither limit its strength nor put a limit to its range. This it is that strikes me most. I have often thought of it. This it is that proves to me conclusively the divinity of Jesus Christ!"

DEFENSE ATTY: Do you wish to cross-examine the witness?

PROS. ATTY: No questions.

DEFENSE ATTY: Your Honor, the defense rests.

JUDGE: Mr. Prosecuting Attorney, are you ready to present your final argument to the jury?

PROS. ATTY: Yes, Your Honor.

JUDGE: Proceed.

PROS. ATTY: Ladies and gentlemen of the jury, you've heard the evidence, and I think you will say that the issue is clear. Either Jesus is the Christ, the Son of God, and so should be acquitted of any blasphemy; or he is an impostor and a deceiver who made such claims he could not substantiate, and so should be put to death in the hearts and minds of men.

We have striven to prove to you that he did make such claims as no mere man dare make in this land of reason. The words, "No man spake as this man spake," are true in more senses than one. Such claims are well-nigh unknown in history. We've proven that he claimed to be equal with God; that in saying he had a relationship to God that no man had ever sustained or could

Jn. 7:46

48

sustain were he not deity. We proved that he said he Note 1 F was preexistent. He said he had lived before Abraham lived. When he was praying in the garden, he spoke as though he had known glory with the Lord "before the world was." Thus he made Bethlehem not a birth—but Jn. 17:3 merely an advent—the taking on of human form by one who had lived before the foundation of the world. Now I ask you, is that not a claim to being God? We've also proven unequivocally that when he was cornered on the porch of Solomon's temple he claimed to be the Christ, and they deemed him guilty of blasphemy. Jn. 10:23–31 Caiaphas, the High Priest, stated that under the most holy oath Jesus said he would come in his glory with his angels, and they condemned him guilty of blasphemy.

Pontius Pilate stated that the sentence of death was based on the fact that Jesus claimed kingship and deity. Else, why the cross on the hill?

(If the optional part of the Priest is included in the production, the following paragraph should be part of the Prosecuting Attorney's closing speech. As optional, it is printed in italics.)

(PROS. ATTY:) *Then you remember how at the Feast of Tabernacles, when the High Priest was carrying that* See Part Three, F *empty pitcher, he said that if they believed on him, the Spirit would fill their thirsty hearts with his living water. What an arrogant offer! What a blasphemous promise for anyone to make if he were not divine.*

So there is nothing for you to do, I say as Unbelief, but to condemn him in the rooms of your minds and to accuse him of blasphemy. The only alternative is to crown him, which I, Unbelief, ask you not to do. Thank you, Your Honor.

JUDGE: Mr. Attorney for the Defense, are you ready with your rebuttal?

DEFENSE ATTY: I am, sir.

JUDGE: Proceed.

DEFENSE ATTY: Ladies and gentlemen of the jury, this is no passing question before you today. "Once to every man and nation comes the moment to decide, In this fight twixt truth and falsehood, for the good or evil side." Jesus of Nazareth is on trial for the crime of blasphemy. Now, blasphemy, as the Honorable Judge will undoubtedly define it for you, is that expression of man's mind which takes to itself outwardly the attributes of God without possessing them. The prosecution has endeavored to prove to you that Jesus claimed to be God and have the attributes of God. This we do not deny; this, we too, affirm. We do not wish to establish the innocence of Jesus by endeavoring to prove he never made such claims. We endeavor to establish his innocence by proving that he is God and that these claims could be confirmed. Review the evidence swiftly.

Mary of Bethany proved to you beyond a peradventure of a doubt that he raised her brother, Lazarus, from the dead.

Nicodemus, against a background that would have made him very prejudiced against anyone who claimed to be the Messiah, admitted that both he and his compeers admitted this man came from God, for no one else did the miracles he did. The woman of Samaria told you how he looked through her very life and revealed her secrets. Was not this the prerogative of God?

The centurion whose heart had been hardened by the deaths of a thousand men stood there and cried, "This was the Son of God!" And even the military is persuaded.

J. R. Lowell

Note 1 A

Note 2

Note 1 H

Note 10

50

Saul of Tarsus went into the book of experience. He showed that Jesus did for him what only a God could do. He could say, "Once I was and now I am," and you cannot dissolve experience even in the acids of unbelief. Womanhood told you how he had set her free. Is not he the God of deliverance? Napoleon, the emperor, said he had no other explanation for this imperishable empire of Jesus Christ save that divinity dwelt within him. Now it is not for his sake that I ask you to acquit him. You cannot harm him; you cannot touch him. For two thousand years men have been digging his grave, but he has always walked out. Why, the points of the shaft of unbelief have been blunted against the shield of faith, and all the darts of skepticism have fallen spent at the feet of truth. Why even those who blaspheme him merely call his name to memory, and his name is everywhere. It is for your own sakes that I ask you to acquit him, that you in acquitting may acquit your own hearts of unbelief and wrong.

Jn. 3:36; 5:24; 8:24

(If the optional part of the Priest is included in the production, the following paragraphs will be the conclusion of the Defense Attorney's closing speech. As optional, they are printed in italics.)

Let you witnesses who have so clearly and courageously defended this Galilean in this courtroom not hate or despise those who condemn him. Even in his agony on the cross he cried, "Father, forgive them, they know not what they do."

See Part Three

Lk. 23:34

Let us be thankful for so many of his own race who have followed him. The Jewish nation gave us our Savior. You and I who are Christians work full-time for a Jew. Thank God for this gift of a Savior from the tribe of Judah. The Jews gave us the commandments

51

*and the prophets upon which much more of our mo-
rality rests, or should rest. God's greatest gift to the
world was his Son, who became incarnate, born in the
flesh, of a woman—a Jewess named Mary, the channel
and instrument of that gift.*

*The Christian church at its birth owed itself largely
to Jews who founded it and accepted Christ as their
Messiah. Many of them became our first missionaries.
Nearly all of the New Testament was penned by the
Holy Spirit through the quills and styluses of this race
—through Matthew, Mark, Paul, Peter and James.
Christ saw fit to portray his majestic program for to-
morrow through John in his revelation.*

*But we have heard how many of these Jews were in-
strumental in applying pressure that helped bring about
Jesus' crucifixion and death. Admitted, but so did you
and I of the defense. Each time we call Jesus Lord, and
sin, we "crucify our Lord afresh and put him to open
shame"; daily we need his cross of forgiveness and redemption.*

Hb. 6:6

*Certainly we cannot approve of what his enemies
said and are saying about him. But remember this!
Love is not approval—love is concern. Therefore as this
trial goes on in each generation, may we who testify in
word and deed be fervently, earnestly and lovingly concerned that our hearers be willing to try filling their
pitchers with that living water we have tested and
found sufficient for our thirst and our faith. We are not
fighting their religion. We are offering to fulfill it
through concerned Christianity.*

*All of us are the jury. There can be no neutrality. We
all must hand in our verdicts. Either Jesus Christ is the
Son of God, and we must kneel and say, "My Lord and
my God," or we condemn him in our minds and hearts
as a blasphemer.*

Jn. 20:28

Either we convict him as a great impostor or we crown him emperor in our hearts. And I beg you to crown him that you may reign with him.

(At this point, the Defense Attorney's final speech concludes, if the part of the Priest is included. If the part of the Priest is omitted, the speech picks up here for the final paragraph.)

There is destiny in this question. This man said, "If ye believe not that I am he, ye shall die in your sins." All heaven is waiting breathlessly on your decision. If you believe he was not the Son of God you must kill him the second time, this time in the hearts and minds of men. But if you believe him to be the Son of God, then you must crown him Emperor in your soul. And I beg of you, in the name of reason and of right, that you crown him, that you may reign with him.

Jn. 8:21–24; 7:33–34

Thank you, Your Honor.

JUDGE: Ladies and gentlemen of the jury, I would remind you, in this court of fairness and justice, of your sacred obligation. Never was there a verdict which so affected the lives of countless people. What you do today is quite inseparable from the lot of millions.

The case has been clearly defined. This man is on trial for blasphemy. Blasphemy consists of taking to oneself the attributes of God without actually possessing them. It is making the declarations which bring God down to the level of man or lift men up to the level of God. If this defendant is a mere man, his claims are such as should lead you to convict him. In condemning Jesus, you are stating that the scholars who, having examined the evidence, believed on him, were not wise but deluded men. You would thus condemn every word the defendant spoke as being devoid of authority. Any man who would deceive you concerning himself would also deceive you concerning yourselves. If he were wrong here, he might be wrong everywhere. If on the other hand, you believe this man, in the face of evidence and experience, to be God, then you must acquit him, and you must do it decisively and fearlessly.

May I remind you of the necessary implications of acquitting him. In saying he is divine, you leave this place declaring you must treat him as divine. You cannot leave this courtroom saying he is divine without worshiping him. Refusing to crucify him as a blasphemer, you must crown him as your King! If he be God, then his every desire is a law in your life. If he be God, then he maps out for you the course of calling of your lives. If he be God, then you must live your lives guiding your actions and your standards by the art of keeping your eye on his face, on his life. If he be God and you thus acquit him today, you must love him to the death! You take your stand with these witnesses, and as they gave their testimony at the risk of their lives, so you cast your lot with them in willingness to sacrifice yours.

Note 1 E

If the claims of this man be true, then he himself shall someday judge the world. Then, in a greater courtroom than this, with a greater Judge than I, a mere man, you and I, all of us, shall stand before him and he shall have the scepter in his hand.

Today the decision is yours. He stands before everyone. What will you do with Jesus? Tomorrow the question shall be his: What shall I do with these? I charge you in the name of Reason, Truth, Light, and Life to weigh carefully your verdict. For yourselves and for innumerable other souls, destiny lies in your decision.

What will you do with Jesus?

(Optional hymn or solo: "What will you do with Jesus?")

What Will You Do With Jesus?

Anon.   M. L. STOCKS

1. Je - sus is stand-ing in Pi-late's hall—Friendless, for-sak-en, be-trayed by all:
2. Je - sus is stand-ing on tri - al still, You can be false to Him if you will,
3. Will you e-vade Him as Pi-late tried? Or will you choose Him, what-e'er be-tide?
4. Will you, like Peter, your Lord de-ny? Or will you scorn from His foes to fly,
5. "Je - sus, I give Thee my heart to-day! Je - sus, I'll fol - low Thee all the way,

Heark-en! what mean-eth the sud-den call! What will you do with Je - sus?
You can be faith-ful thro' good or ill: What will you do with Je - sus?
Vain - ly you strug-gle from Him to hide: What will you do with Je - sus?
Dar - ing for Je - sus to live or die? What will you do with Je - sus?
Glad - ly o - bey-ing Thee!" will you say: "This will I do with Je - sus!"

CHORUS

What will you do with Je - sus? Neu-tral you can - not be;

Some day your heart will be ask - ing, "What will He do with me?"

Production
Suggestions

Staging

The *judge* should be seated on a center elevation, presiding at a table. If the drama is presented in the main church sanctuary, he can be seated in the central choir section behind a railing. He should be easily visible at all times.

The *bailiff* should be at one end of the platform with a small table beside him for easy reference to the list of witnesses.

The two *attorneys* can sit together or at two tables set at approximately right angles to the audience and in a position so that they can easily address the bench. There should be space at the table ends to allow them to leave and approach the witness stand for their questioning.

If the play is performed in the church sanctuary, the *witness stand* can be the pulpit or lectern placed at an angle to face both the audience (jury) and the two attorneys. The witnesses should enter from offstage as the bailiff summons them. After testifying, they may be seated in the auditorium, on the front row, to avoid having the audience's attention focused on them rather than on the witness on stage.

A vacant chair between the two attorneys symbolizes the presence of the *defendant,* Jesus of Nazareth. (Note the judge's opening remarks on the defendant's invisible presence.)

If the church, hall, or auditorium is large, great care should be taken to make microphones conveniently available to the cast. Stationary microphones can be used for the judge, bailiff, and witnesses. The two attorneys need lapel or other microphones to permit their mobility as they address the judge, jury, and witnesses. The use of the cassette "Christ on Trial" (see page 11, footnote 2) is an invaluable coaching aid.

Costuming

Some casts play their parts in modern dress for convenience' sake—except for the judge, who wears a robe.

However, there is a vital translation of the audience to a first-century atmosphere when period costumes are used. Helpful authentic suggestions can be garnered from the photograph of the professional Hollywood cast that follows these suggestions. Groups, clubs and churches often reveal surprising expertise for this costuming task.

Closing

Some have found it effective to follow the closing charge of the judge with music, either a congregational hymn or a solo. Optional music is printed at the end of the drama.

Permission to Produce

As noted on the copyright page, purchase of this book does not convey the right to put on the play in

any form. Permission to produce the play must be obtained in writing from Word Books, Publisher, 4800 West Waco Drive, Waco, TX 76703. This will be granted on a non-royalty basis, contingent upon purchase of four copies of the book. Three of these copies will be needed for the parts of the Judge, the Attorney for the Prosecution, and the Attorney for the Defense; the fourth copy may be torn apart to provide individual parts for the witnesses and for the first speech of the bailiff. The bailiff's announcements of the successive witnesses may readily be learned without a written part, or may easily be copied out from one of the four purchased books.

Opposite page: Cast of characters in costume for a presentation of *The People versus Jesus*. Top row, left to right: Bailiff, Dr. Clifton E. Moore; Nicodemus, John Merton; Saul of Tarsus, Dennis Morgan; the Woman of Samaria, Rhonda Fleming; Attorney for the Defense, Mr. Reasonable Faith, Dr. Louis H. Evans, Sr.; Judge, The Honorable Fairness, Bill Hay; Prosecuting Attorney, Mr. Frank Unbelief, John Holland; Caiaphas, James Logan; a Pharisee, Murray F. Barnard; the Centurion, Henry Wilcoxin. Bottom row, left to right: Napoleon, Porter Hall; Womanhood, Geraldine Hall; Pontius Pilate, Michael O'Shea; Mary of Bethany, Virginia Mayo; Keeper of the Garden, George Chandler.

Part Two
THE NOTES

Introduction
Why These Notes?

So stupendous and deep and far-reaching are the claims made by Jesus Christ and Christianity, that the believer, and the searcher, have been and will be faced with denials, questions and opposition. This was both explained and prophesied in Peter's second epistle: "False prophets also arose among the people, just as there will be false teachers among you, who will secretly bring in destructive heresies, even denying the Master who bought them. . . . Many will follow their licentiousness, and because of them the way of truth will be reviled. And in their greed [their love for money and gain] they will exploit you with false words; from of old their condemnation has not been idle, and their destruction has not been asleep. . . . Bold and wilful, they are not afraid to revile the glorious ones. . . . They entice unsteady souls. They have hearts trained in greed. . . . Therefore, beloved, knowing this beforehand, beware lest you be carried away by the error of lawless men and lose your own stability. But grow in the grace and knowledge of our Lord and Savior Jesus Christ."

2 Pe. 2:1–3, 10, 14; 3:17–18, RSV

In many areas of the world today, through the faith and faithfulness of witnessing there has been a great resurgence of conversions to Christ, so much so that many feel the enemy is "getting out all his guns" and with new zeal using every device to counter this movement of the Spirit toward Christ. This is being done unabashedly and unashamedly on the screen, in the classroom, at the lectern and in the press. Often, as Peter suggests, it is done from greed—some believing that in literature "the best smellers make the best sellers." One film portrays the Lord as a homosexual; another a faker of miracles; another claims he never said he was the Son of God, etc.

A part of the solution to this moral and theological collapse lies in the admonition, "Study to show yourself approved unto God, a workman who does not need to be ashamed and confused, rightly dividing the word of truth." The word translated "dividing" is a physician's word (*orthotomounta*), meaning to cut straight, precisely and carefully. In operating, a doctor must know the difference between diseased and healthy flesh as he uses his scalpel—and a writer had better know the difference between truth and error as he uses his pen, or he can in his greed for royalties injure the human soul. Believing is life; unbelief is spiritual death.

Books, films and talk can make or break one's faith. False talk will eat away like gangrene. Choose a book like you would choose a friend. "Shun profane and vain babblings: for they will increase unto more ungodliness. . . . Among them are Hymenaeus and Philetus, who have swerved from the truth by holding that the resurrection is past already. They are upsetting the faith of some. But God's firm foundation stands."

The material in Part Two is the result of careful research—biblical, historical, scientific and medical. It also includes the opinions of many types of reliable scholars. Some of the notes have to do with the jurisprudence, both Roman and Jewish, of Christ's day. They also include the testimony of leading scholars of our day as to the person of Christ and to pertinent events in his life.

2 Tm. 2:15, lit.

2 Tm. 2:16–19, KJV, RSV

64

Note 1.

The Claims of Christ

A. The Son of God

God was uniquely his Father. "But Jesus answered   Jn. 5:17–18,
them, My Father worketh hitherto, and I work. There-   KJV
fore the Jews sought the more to kill him, because he
not only had broken the sabbath, but said also that
God was his Father—making himself equal with God."
The Greek word translated *his* is *idion,* the most intensive pronoun in the language. It is translated in the
lexicon as "one's own—peculiar to—that which belongs
specifically to one—as one's own wife, property—private, individual."

Christ was indicating that God was his own Father—
belonging to him in a special way, "thus making himself *equal* [*ison*] with God." Other translators bring out
the meaning in various ways.

Goodspeed—"thus putting himself on an equality
with God."

Weymouth—"spoke of God as being in a special
sense His Father, thus putting Himself on a level with
God."

Moffatt—"actually spoke of God as his own Father,
thereby making himself equal to God."

Phillips—"he referred to God as his own Father, so
putting himself on equal terms with God."

65

B. Only Begotten Son

Only begotten means the only begotten of God—the only one born this way. He, God from the beginning, became incarnate in the flesh as the son of Mary, but as the Son of man he was still identical with the Son of God. This was by the miracle of the Holy Spirit through which she gave birth to the divine Son of man. It is not true that Christ only referred to himself as the Son of man—he used this interchangeably with Son of God.

Jn. 3:16, KJV

"God so loved the world that he gave his only begotten Son." Like begets like. An animal begets an animal. A man begets a man. God created man, he did not beget him. When Christ was born in the flesh he was begotten of God—God begets God. *Only* Christ was born this way. Christ spoke of himself as *the*, not *a*, Son of man, meaning that he was unique.

Mt. 16:13–18, RSV

When Christ asked who the disciples thought he, the Son of man, was, Peter replied, "Christ, the Son of the living God." Jesus replied that "my Father who is in heaven . . . revealed this to you." So, then, "the Son of man" is identical to "the Son of God." In the Greek, Jesus always uses the definite rather than the indefinite article or none at all. " 'For the Father himself loves you, because you have loved me and have believed that I came from the Father. I came from the Father and have come into the world; again, I am leaving the world and going to the Father.' His disciples said, 'Ah, now you are speaking plainly, not in any figure!' " From the evidence of these two verses, it is difficult to claim that by calling himself the Son of man Jesus is saying he is not the Son of God.

Jn. 16:27–28, RSV

Some answer, "But are we not all 'sons of God'?" Certainly, but not in Christ's unique way. There is a new spiritual relationship that we do attain when by acceptance of Jesus Christ we become the children of

66

1. The Claims of Christ

God, but children by *adoption*—not birth. "But as many as received him [Christ], to them he gave power to *become* children of God, even to them that believe on his name." Here the word for children is *tekna* which can mean adopted child. By the act of believing we receive this adoption into the family of God by faith, and *become* what we were not *originally*—children of God. "God so loved the world that he gave his only begotten *Son*." The Greek word used here for "Son" is not *teknon* but *huios* which means an *original* flesh-and-blood son.

Jn. 1:12, KJV

Jn. 3:16, KJV

C. The Messiah

Some scholars say that Christ never himself made the claim to messiahship, that is, that he was the Redeemer, the Deliverer, who would set Israel free.

Messiah was the Hebrew name by which he would be known. It is a word meaning "anointed one." *Christ* comes from the Greek word *Christos*, which has the same meaning and refers to the same person. Andrew learned this as a pupil of his teacher, John the Baptist, at his seminar in the desert. Upon returning home, he immediately found his brother, Simon Peter, and told him, "We have found the Messiah," (which means Christ) and he led him to Jesus. The Christ and the Messiah are two names for the same person.

Jn. 1:35–42, RSV

Did Jesus claim to be the Messiah? During his conversation with the woman of Samaria, she said to him, " 'I know that Messiah is coming (he who is called Christ). . . .' Jesus said to her, 'I who speak to you am he.' " This is a clear identification on Jesus' part as to his being the Messiah. So is Martha's answer of belief to Jesus' statement "I am the resurrection and the life. . . . Do you believe this?": "Yes, Lord! I do believe that you are the Messiah, the Son of God, who was to come into the world."

Jn. 4:25–26, RSV

Jn. 11:26–27, TEV

D. Christ as Savior

Lk. 2:10–11, RSV

We hear that the Christ is called a Savior in the announcement of his birth by the angel: "Be not afraid; for behold, I bring you good news of a great joy which will come to all the people; for to you is born this day in the city of David a *Savior*, who is Christ the Lord."

Mt. 9:6, RSV

Jesus claimed the powers of a Savior. When the religious leaders got angry because he pronounced forgiveness to a sick man, he said to them, " 'But that you may know that the Son of man has authority on earth to forgive sins'—he then said to the paralytic—'Rise, take up your bed and go home.' " Mark adds, "They were all amazed and glorified God, saying, 'We never saw anything like this!' "

Mk. 2:11, 12, RSV

Mt. 1:22, RSV

The Apostles proclaimed it. Matthew included it in his account of Jesus' birth. ". . . and you shall call his name Jesus, for he will *save* his people from their sins."

1 Jn. 4:14, RSV

John wrote, "And we have seen and testify that the Father sent his Son as the Savior of the world."

2 Pe. 3:2, RSV

Peter told us, "You should remember the predictions of the holy prophets and the commandment of the Lord and Savior through your apostles."

E. Christ—Judge of the World

Scripture and the apostles declare that Jesus Christ will one day judge the world. "[God] has fixed a day on which he will judge the world in righteousness by a man whom he has appointed, and of this he has given assurance to all men by raising him from the dead." Easter is the stamp of God on the judgeship of Jesus.

Ac. 17:31, RSV

Christ will come to "judge the alive and the dead."

Ac. 10:42, RSV

"He [Christ] is the one ordained by God to be judge of the living and the dead."

2 Co. 5:10, KJV

"We must all appear before the judgment seat of Christ."

68

1. The Claims of Christ

Christ himself claimed it. "For judgment I came into this world." — Jn. 9:39, RSV

"The Father judges no one, but has given all judgment to the Son, that all may honor the Son, even as they honor the Father who sent him. He who does not honor the Son does not honor the Father who sent him." — Jn. 5:22–23, RSV

F. Preexistence

In John's vision, Christ says of himself, "I am Alpha and Omega, the beginning and the ending." — Rv. 1:8, KJV

Jesus told the Jewish leaders, "Before Abraham was *I am*." I AM was the name of God revealed to Moses. Rehearse from the play the claims of Jesus for which the Jews tried to stone him—the testimony of the Pharisee. Compare John 8:58 with Exodus 3:14. "I AM" is God. — Jn. 8:58 Ex. 3:13–14 See also Jn. 5:17 ff.

Read Christ's statement about his own history. "I came forth from the Father, and am come into the world: again I leave the world, and go to the Father." — Jn. 16:28, KJV

G. Oneness with God

"I and my Father are one" Jesus said of himself. He was one in essence with the Father. "The Father is in union with me" (Williams). "I am in union with the Father" (Goodspeed). — Jn. 10:30, KJV; see vv. 31–33 Jn. 10:38

"The Father is in me and I am in the Father" (RSV; see also KJV).

H. Worked Miracles

A word of explanation may be helpful about the miracles of Jesus. There are different words translated "miracle" in the New Testament.

1. *Dunamis,* from which we get our word *dynamite,*

indicates some supernatural act performed to demonstrate some *power* possessed by the one performing it. This power was sometimes used negatively and was demonic and deceitful. Simon the sorceror used it to Ac. 8:11 deceive the people. In Revelation 13:11–14 the Beast Rv. 13:11–14 uses such miracles to deceive. Sometimes these powerful works are done for a Christian purpose—to substantiate the authority of the message being brought. Ac. 6:8 / 1 Co. 12:9 Stephen used this power for the glory of Christ. Paul names this miraculous power as one of the gifts of the Ac. 9:11 Holy Spirit. He himself used it to cast out demons and also to heal the sick in the name of the Lord Jesus.

2. *Erga*, meaning "works" is also used to refer to miracles. The miracles or good works call our attention to the *object* which is blessed, the person helped, like Mt. 11:2–5 the miracles of healing performed by Christ which Jm. 2:14–16 John the Baptist heard of. The generous works which James refers to, when the hungry are fed and the naked are clothed, indicate that such works, though not necessarily miracles, should accompany our Christian faith as evidence of our sincerity.

Ac. 6:8 3. *Terata* is another word for miracles and is transAc. 15:12 lated "wonders" in Acts 6:8 of the works of Stephen. Paul and Barnabas supported their account of their ministry by calling attention to these acts of *unusual power* God had performed through them. The word calls attention to miracles as evidence.

4. *Sēmeia* is probably the most usual word for miracles and is often translated "signs." These miracles point us primarily, not to the power it took to work the miracle or the advantage to the recipient, but to the *authority of the one performing the miracles* or to the one in whose name the miracle was performed. These Rv. 16:14, KJV miracles, too, can be used in an evil way, by "the spirits of devils, working miracles," and by false prophets to Rv. 19:20 win followers to themselves. Christ most often used the sign or miracle *to establish his divine nature, source,*

1. The Claims of Christ

and character. By signs, Christ to a great degree established his deity and won his great following. This greatly troubled his antagonists, the chief priests and Pharisees. After he raised Lazarus from the dead, they said, "This man performs many signs. If we let him go on thus, every one will believe in him." Later they admitted that they could do nothing against him, because "the whole world has gone after him."

Jn. 11:47–48; 12:19, RSV

Note how Jesus used signs to establish his divine attributes and nature. The miracle of the multiplication of the loaves enabled him to prove that he is "the living bread which came down from heaven." Christ dared to say, "I am the light of the world." To prove this he healed the blind man, thus showing his power to change the spiritual darkness into spiritual light. Many believed this sign. The cured man himself said, " 'Lord, I believe'; and he worshiped him."

Jn. 6
Jn. 8:12; 9:1–41

Jn. 9:38, RSV

Christ used the sign of the resurrection of Lazarus to prove he could say, "I am the resurrection and the life."

Note 2

Jesus definitely declared that his miraculous signs proved he was the true Messiah. When John the Baptist languished in his prison cell, Jesus did not use power to release him. John, discouraged, felt he might have placed his faith in the wrong man as the Messiah, that perhaps he had been taken in and deceived. So he asked the disciples to ask this frankly of Jesus, "Are you he who is come or do we look for another?" Jesus sent back his answer, "Go and tell John what you hear and see: the blind receive their sight, the lame walk, lepers are cleansed and the deaf hear, and the dead are raised up. . . . And blessed is he who takes no offense at me."

Mt. 11:2–6, RSV

Nicodemus the Pharisee and ruler of the Jews said to Jesus, "Rabbi [Teacher] we [even some of us Jewish leaders] know that you are a teacher come from God, and *no man* [nobody else—Greek, *oudeis*] can do the signs you do unless *God be with him.*"

Jn. 3:1–2, RSV, itals added

Some critics say that Jesus bowed to the ignorance

of a prescientific era and pretended to perform supernatural works. But who would want to follow a leader
who tried to prove his deity by such vicious deceit! He
would thus be utterly dishonest, unworthy of honest
followers. Yet the disciples and thousands of honest
men did follow him and believe. It was these indisputable signs that spurred dishonest religious leaders to
call a council and say, " 'What are we to do? For this
man performs many signs. If we let him go on thus,
every one will believe in him.' . . . they took counsel
how to put him to death."

Jn. 11:47,
53, RSV

Note 2.

Was Lazarus Really Dead?

The miracle of Christ's raising Lazarus from the dead was very convincing to the many citizens of Bethany who witnessed it. It is recorded in John that as a result of Lazarus's coming out of the tomb at Christ's command, "many of the Jews therefore, who had come with Mary and had seen what he did, believed in him; but some of them went to the Pharisees and told them what Jesus had done."

Jn. 11:45, RSV

(a) Martha, Lazarus's sister, brought out the fact in the conversation at the tomb that it was evident Lazarus was dead and therefore the situation was hopeless. When Jesus said to take away the stone, Martha said to him, "Lord, by this time he stinketh: for he hath been dead four days." Jesus said to her unflinchingly, "Did I not tell you that if you would believe you would see the glory of God?" Before this Jesus had definitely said, "Lazarus is dead," in answer to the supposition that by saying "he has fallen asleep," people would think he would merely raise him from a coma.

Jn. 11:39, KJV

Jn. 11:40, RSV
Jn. 11:14, 11, RSV

History tells us that many rabbis and physicians agreed that after a body had been dead—without respiration or pulse—for four days and there was the definite odor of bodily disintegration and putrefaction, this definitely established the person's verifiable death.

73

There was no question that day that Lazarus was truly dead, and that it was an unquestioned miracle that brought him back to life.

Jn. 11:52; 12:9-11

From this time on the Jewish rulers planned to kill Lazarus, this living evidence, as well as Christ.

Jn. 11:42, RSV,

(b) In his prayer to the Father before he raised Lazarus, Jesus said he was asking for this power "that they may believe that thou didst send me." He laid the

Jn. 11:25

foundation for this by saying earlier, "I am the resurrection and the life." He who changed physical death into life could also conquer spiritual death—which is the separation of a soul from God. Now the religious leaders must find a means of doing away with both—Lazarus, who stood there as living proof of this miraculous sign, and Jesus, who had the supernatural power to perform it.

Note 3.

The Arrest in the Garden

(a) Why the arrest at night, in a garden? *Jerusalem and its environs were upset religiously and politically.* The Galilean peasant named Jesus was the cause of the unrest. He had made blasphemous claims in the eyes of many—claims to deity, to being "one with God," pre-existent. He claimed to be the King that would come in the name of the Lord; the son of David yet the Lord of David; the Messiah who was to come. Sitting on a colt he accepted the plaudits of the crowd—their high-held palm branches and their cloaks thrown in his royal way.

The movement for this Messiah was swelling.

Thousands had rallied to his messages on the hills, in the synagogues, in the towns and cities, at the hearthsides and the seashores. Many were leaving their vocations to follow him.

His indisputable miracles were dismaying his enemies—the multitudes were fed, the lame walked, the blind had sight, and the dead lived. At Bethany, at his command, Lazarus had come to life again and many in Bethany saw and believed. They had found their resurrection and their life. The chief priests were angry and now "they planned to put Lazarus to death because on account of him many of the Jews were going away and believing on Jesus." Jn. 12:2–11

Jn. 12:10, RSV

75

These and other events incensed the religious leaders. Christ had verbally chastised the scribes and Pharisees and called some of them hypocrites and whitewashed tombs. He had made havoc of their peace of mind. At a gathering of the Pharisees they said one to another,

Jn. 12:19, RSV

"You see that you can do nothing; look, the world has gone after him." And they began subtle planning for Jesus' arrest.

There were problems. Should they dare to arrest

Mk. 14:1–2

Christ before the eyes of that festival crowd that would gather for the Passover at Jerusalem? Many of his friends would be there—would not the effect be catastrophic in the rioting it would cause? It must be done quietly, "subtly," out of sight and sound of the people at the feast. "Then the chief priests and elders of the people gathered in the palace of the high priest, who was called Caiaphas, and took counsel together in order

Mt. 26:3, RSV

to arrest Jesus by stealth and kill him. But they said, 'Not during the feast, lest there be a tumult among the people.'"

Their problem was solved when one of the twelve disciples, Judas Iscariot, went to the high priests.

Mt. 26:15, RSV

"'What will you give me if I deliver him to you?' And they paid him thirty pieces of silver." Judas could lead them to that quiet spot on the Mount of Olives where Jesus was accustomed to rest and pray in the evenings.

On the night of his arrest, Jesus went there again quietly to pray through the facing of the cross. The disciples were with him and he took three of them apart to pray with him, and went on further to pray by himself. Then stealthily came the motley assortment of arresters.

Mt. 26:47
Mk. 14:43
Lk. 22:47

(b) Who were they? The various words used to describe them are in agreement in the Gospels. (Read Matt. 26:47–56; Mark 14:43–52; Luke 22:47–53; and John 18:1–12.) There was a great (Matt.) *multitude*

3. The Arrest in the Garden

(KJV) or *crowd* (RSV; *ochlos polus*)—a large number of
people with swords and staves or clubs. Christ, either
humorously or caustically, asked why it took so many
to arrest a single unarmed man. John identifies the
crowd. "So Judas, procuring a band [*speiron*] of soldiers
and some officers [*hupēretai*] from the chief priests
and the Pharisees, went there with lanterns and torches
and weapons." Luke refers to the *captains* (KJV) or
"*officers of the temple* [*stratēgous tou hierou*] and elders who had come out against him." According to
Mark, the crowd was sent by or came "from the chief
priest and the scribes and the elders." Also in the arresting party were the slaves of the high priests. Peter, who
was aroused from prayer by the commotion of the
crowd's arrival, "having a sword, drew it and struck the
high priest's slave [*doulos*, servant or slave] and cut off
his right ear."

Jn. 18:3, RSV

Lk. 22:52, RSV

Mk. 14:43, RSV

Jn. 18:10, RSV

It is apparent that the arresting party was composed
of leaders and officers in their employ—Jewish police,
The Living Bible calls them, or temple police (according to Dr. James Stewart).[1]

It is also evident that this arrest was planned, paid
for and executed by Caiaphas and the Jewish rulers.

There is no evidence that previous to the arrest Pilate
had any knowledge or part of it. A few scholars, however, do contend that a few Roman soldiers might have
been present at the arrest, but most feel that it would
have been an insult to Roman soldiers to send several
of them to arrest a humble unarmed peasant such as
Jesus of Nazareth. And would officers and personnel of
the holy temple be seen in the company of despised
Gentile military who had already defiled the temple
with their arms and standards? Another point: this

---

1. *The Life and Teachings of Christ* (Nashville: Abingdon
Press, 1958), p. 156.

Jn. 18:12–13
Mt. 26:57,
59, RSV
Mk. 14:55,
RSV

arresting mob did not bring Jesus to Pilate but to the house of the High Priest who had planned the arrest (having stopped off first at the house of Annas, ex-High Priest, Caiaphas's father-in-law). Here the Sanhedrin was to have its impromptu and hurried meeting at night. Matthew and Mark both state that "the whole council" was there, and several versions translate "council" as "Sanhedrin" (*The Jerusalem Bible*, the Berkeley version, and others). The first trial will be not Roman but Jewish, not political but theological.

Note 4.

The Theological Trials of Jesus

A. The Sanhedrin

The Sanhedrin was the supreme judicial council of the Jews, especially for religious affairs. For the Jews, however, there was no distinction between civil and religious affairs. Therefore, into the hands of this Sanhedrin was placed supreme authority in all things: (1) they interpreted the law; (2) they appointed sacred rites; (3) they imposed tributes; (4) they decreed war; (5) they judged in capital offenses—in short, they were engrossed in and responsible for the supreme authority in legislative, judicial and executive areas.

On those guilty of crimes they could even pronounce sentence of death. However, under Roman rule, they were not permitted to carry out the execution of the death sentence; their power ended with the judgment or decision. The sentence was then transmitted to the Roman procurator with whom it rested—to execute or not as he chose.

Composition. The Sanhedrin was composed of seventy or seventy-two members chosen from among the people. They were called judges and consisted of the most eminent elders, priests, scribes, and Pharisees. They held office for life. Frequently, providing he was

Jn. 18:31;
Mt. 27:1–21

a man endowed with wisdom, the High Priest was a member of the Sanhedrin. The office of president belonged to the High Priest (if a member) and it was his prerogative to summon the council together and preside over its deliberations.

Protocol. The council usually sat in a semicircle. The president occupied the center, a scribe at each extremity—their duty to record the sentences pronounced by the council. They usually met in a hall close by the Great Gate of the Temple near the Holy Place, or the Hall of Hewn Stone. In cases of emergency the council might be convened in the house of the High Priest.

Mt. 26:3

There were strict laws governing their meeting. They were not to meet after sundown. One complete day should pass after a death sentence, doubtless to allow time for thoughtful consideration as to the validity of the decision. No man could be legally tried without a witness in his behalf. Public announcement was to be made regarding meetings to avoid secret or devious acts of the council apart from the people.

There are examples of breaches of that protocol in several places in the Bible. In the case of James, the brother of Jesus, the historian Josephus says that after the death of Festus and before the arrival of his successor, the High Priest Annas availed himself of this opportunity to condemn James and others to death by stoning. This sentence was carried out and subsequently viewed with great displeasure by the new procurator, Albinus, with the result that Annas was expelled from the office of High Priest (*Antiquities,* 22:9–11).

Ac. 7:58

Stephen, the brave Christian martyr, was stoned during the absence of the Roman procurator.

The Smaller Sanhedrin. Talmudical writers say that, in addition to the Sanhedrin, there was in every town containing not fewer than 150 people a smaller San-

4. The Theological Trials of Jesus

hedrin of fifteen or twenty members before which lesser cases were tried, whose decisions could be appealed to the large council.

But Jesus was not brought before the smaller Sanhedrin, because the Scripture agrees that "all" or "the whole" council met that first evening of his arrest in the house of Caiaphas.

Mt. 26:59, Mk. 14:55, KJV, RSV

We have already noted the claims of Jesus to be the Messiah, the Lamb of God, the Son of God, on an equality with God, and the miracles and signs he had performed and his growing popularity with a great many of the people—all of which irked and worried the religious leaders. How early the wheels of "justice" began to turn we are not sure.

Was the proper "Man Wanted" notice posted? The Babylonian Talmud, according to some Jewish authorities, stipulates that this "wanted" announcement had been issued: "WANTED: YESHU Hannosri [Jesus of Nazareth]. He shall be stoned because he practiced sorcery and enticed Israel to apostasy. Anyone who can say anything in his favor, let him come forward and plead on his behalf. Anyone who knows where he is, let him declare it to the great Sanhedrin in Jerusalem."

Three times, illegally—without proper witnesses or a trial—they tried to stone him.

Jn. 5:18, 8:59; 10:30–31

B. The Trials During Holy Week

1. The Evening Hearing—Thursday

a. Before Annas
They "led him away to Annas [a retired official often consulted out of respect] first; for he was father-in-law to Caiaphas, which was high priest that same year."

Questions: About Jesus' disciples and teachings.

Jesus' answer: "I have said nothing secretly. . . . Ask those who heard me."

Jn. 18:13, KJV
Jn. 18:19–22

81

The result: An officer hit Jesus for not answering. Annas sent Jesus to Caiaphas.

b. Before Caiaphas

Mt. 26:57, RSV

They "led [Jesus] to Caiaphas the high priest, where the scribes and the elders had gathered."

Mt. 26:59, ital added

Attendance: "Now the chief priests, and elders, and *all* the council, sought false witnesses against Jesus to put him to death."

Mt. 26:61–63, RSV

Accusations: (1) That he said he was "able to destroy the temple"—the witnesses disagreed. Jesus held his peace and said nothing. (2) "Tell us if you are the Christ, the Son of God."

Mt. 26:64, RSV

Answer: ". . . you will see the Son of man seated at the right hand of Power, and coming on the clouds of heaven."

Mk. 14:64–65

Sentence: Guilty of blasphemy and worthy of death. And they mocked him, smote him, spat upon him, and reviled him.

2. The Morning Hearing—Friday

Mt. 27:1, RSV
cf. Mk. 15:1
Lk. 22:66
Lk. 22:67, 70, RSV

Attendance: "When morning came *all* the chief priests and elders of the people took counsel against Jesus . . ."

Accusation: "If you are the Christ, tell us. . . . Are you the Son of God, then?"

Answer: "You say that I am" the Son of God. A strong affirmative.

Lk. 22:71

Sentence: "What further testimony do we need? We have heard it ourselves from his own lips."

Judge Gaynor of the New York Bench said that on one fact all the Gospel narratives agree—that the alleged crime for which Christ was tried and convicted was blasphemy. It was not what he said about the temple or an emperor, but what he said about himself and his divinity.

Some are condemned for what they have done. Jesus

died for who he was. Some die because they are guilty. He died because he was God.

Because the power to carry out a sentence of death lay with Rome alone, Jesus next had to appear before Pilate, the Roman procurator.

Note 5.

The Political Trial
before Pilate

Mt. 27:1-2

It is stated several times in the Gospels that the religious leaders sought to kill Jesus. But only Rome had the power to carry out a death sentence, so they brought Jesus to Pilate. There is no evidence that Pilate had become involved in the case before this time.

After the arrest the "multitude," which we have already defined and identified, brought Jesus first to their own Jewish authorities—Annas, Caiaphas and the Sanhedrin. After they had condemned Jesus to death for

Jn. 18:28–30, RSV

blasphemy, the Sanhedrin brought him to Pilate. Pilate met them outside the palace so they would not be defiled at the Passover. It is quite evident that Pilate was unprepared for them. He began with the query, "What accusation do you bring against this man?" Piqued, they answered, "If this man were not an evildoer we would not have handed him over."

Jn. 18:31–32, RSV

Pilate said to them, "Take him and judge him by your own law"—if these are theological charges you can pass your own sentences. But they had already judged him theologically guilty for making himself the Son of God, the Christ, and had found him worthy of death by Jewish law; now they needed Rome to carry out the sentence.

So they proceeded to drag in political allegations for

5. The Political Trial before Pilate

which Pilate, under Roman law, must condemn or acquit Jesus.

A. The Political Charges

1. "And they began to accuse him, saying, 'We found this man perverting our nation . . . saying that he himself is Christ a King.' And Pilate asked him, 'Are you the King of the Jews?' And he answered him, 'You have said so.'" (You said it—a strong affirmative.) *Lk. 23:2-3, RSV cf. Jn. 18:33-36*

To further clarify and establish this charge, Pilate asked again, "Are you a king then?" and Jesus answered, "My kingship is not of this world: if my kingship were of this world, my servants would fight, that I might not be handed over to the Jews." His was a spiritual kingdom in the hearts of men. *Upon this Pilate sought to release him.* *Jn. 18:36, RSV*

Jn. 18:38-39

2. "We found this man . . . forbidding us to give tribute to Caesar." This was a base lie. Jesus had said, "Show me a coin. Whose likeness and inscription has it?" When they answered, "Caesar's," he told them, "Then render to Caesar the things that are Caesar's." *Lk. 23:1, RSV Lk. 20:20-26, RSV*

B. Pilate's Political Decisions Regarding Christ

"I find no crime in this man." *Lk. 23:4, RSV*
"I find no crime in him." *Jn. 18:38;*
"After examining him before you, . . . I did not find this man guilty of any of your charges against him." *19:4, RSV Lk. 23:14, RSV*
"And they cried out again, 'Crucify him.' And Pilate said to them, 'Why, what evil has he done?'" *Mk. 15:13-14, RSV cf. Lk. 23:22*

C. Pilate Tried to Release Jesus

1. Pilate tried to avoid sentencing Jesus by sending him to Herod for trial, since Jesus came from Galilee. *Lk. 23:6-12*

Lk. 23:15–
18, RSV

2. After the trial before Herod is fruitless, Pilate says, "'Herod . . . sent him back to us. Behold, nothing deserving death has been done by him. I will therefore chastise him and release him.' . . . But they all cried out together, 'Away with this man.'" Sometimes the prospect of a bloody scourging would satisfy a mob, but it failed to appease this one.

3. He gives a choice of releasing Jesus or Barabbas. When Pilate perceived that out of envy the chief priests had stirred up the multitudes to cry for the release of Barabbas and the crucifixion of Jesus, he said to them,

Mt. 27:24,
RSV, marg.

"Why, what evil has he done?" But they were adamant in their demand for Jesus' death. Pilate then exclaimed, "I am innocent of this righteous man's blood."

4. He tries to move them to pity to release Jesus by

Jn. 19:1–6,
RSV

actually carrying out the scourging. Scourging, Roman style, was a brutal and bloody punishment. This plus a cruel crown of thorns, the mocking purple robe, should have made the crowd murmur, "This is sufficient humiliation for a King." But this effort to release Jesus failed too, as the mob cried, "Crucify him, crucify him!" Once more Pilate declared, "Take him yourselves and crucify him, for I find no crime in him."

D. What Moved Pilate to Order the Execution?

1. His Position with Caesar Was Threatened

Pilate's obstinacy and attempts to release Jesus now were met by the opposition's boldest stroke. "The Jews cried out, 'If you release this man, you are not Caesar's

Jn. 19:12,
RSV

friend.'" Why? There are two possible answers:

(a) If he cleared Jesus, he might be accused of aiding a traitor. "Every one who makes himself a king sets himself against Caesar," the Jewish leaders told him. But Pilate in his own mind had already cleared

Jesus of any interfering kingship or treason against Caesar.

(b) Caesar wanted to be on good terms with the Jewish community. Hebrew historians have written of Caesar's desire not to interfere with Israel's conduct of religious affairs, as long as they did not smack of treason against Rome.

It is recorded that Tiberius Caesar had promised the Jews that if they laid down their arms, became obediently subservient to Rome and paid their taxes, then Rome would endeavor to carry out the sentences of Jewry's highest court, the Sanhedrin.

Now might be the time to remind Rome of this promise with their words to Pilate, "We have a law, and by that law he ought to die, because he made himself the Son of God." They had passed the edict unanimously, although illegally, as the play shows. Were they saying, "If you do not carry out this death sentence you are making a liar out of Caesar!"? Now Pilate was afraid and his position was threatened. Dare he defy Caesar's promise and thus lose his place in the choice royal circle called, "Friends of Caesar"? If he could please Caesar by condemning Jesus, then he could still wear on his finger the ring Caesar had placed there, symbolizing that he belonged to this coveted circle. This circle no one left save under private mortal disgrace and public scorn. Pilate will sacrifice his "friendship with Christ" and his courage of conscience for his friendship with Caesar—*amici Caesaris*. But Pilate will lose the right to wear around his heart the "ring of joy" that Christ, Emperor of the World and King of Kings, places there to make us *amici Christus* —friends of Christ.

Jn. 19:7, RSV

2. *Pilate Feared the Multitude*

Pilate was walking on thin ice, because in several

ways he had *already deeply offended the Jews in his realm* and so had irked Caesar.

(a) Both Philo and Josephus record that the Romans paraded into sacred areas of Jerusalem *bearing Roman standards* and medallions deifying Caesar. Jews demonstrated for five days and complained to Caesar. Pilate had them removed, but the harm had been done.

(b) Pilate was accused of taking money from the temple treasury and *using the tribute money* for the construction of his system of aqueducts and cisterns. This also was reported to Caesar, who wrote a fiery letter to Pilate rebuking him for his actions.

(c) There was the *massacre at Mt. Gerizim*. Fearing that a false messiah and magician was leading a movement against Rome, Pilate had sent his soldiers to stop the process. But so strong were the Samaritans worshiping there that a bloody battle ensued and many Samaritans were slaughtered. The Romans had conquered but the Samaritans objected bitterly to the emperor.

(d) Pilate was having *a "bad press."* The desired compromise between Jerusalem and Rome was worsening. On top of that, the visits to Caesar's court of Herod, King of the Jews, who desired his cousin to be procurator in Pilate's stead, were making Pilate's position uncertain.

Mk. 15:11
(e) The unwillingness of Pilate himself to condemn Jesus caused the *chief priests to stir up the multitudes* to condemn Christ and to pressure Pilate. They could do this because in Jerusalem at this time were not only many friends of Christ but also many of the enemies he had incurred: unjust tax collectors he had criticized and scourged from the temple; the religious leaders he had called whitewashed tombs, hypocrites. In addition, one historian has said that there were also in Jerusalem at the Passover season a great many temple soldiers. There were also those who wanted a more militant messiah who would lead them against Rome.

5. The Political Trial before Pilate

E. The Capitulation

Pilate, sensing the forces that had been stirred up against him, took a basin and washed his hands of the responsibility of the forced sentence of death, lacking the courage to withstand the wrath of the religious leaders and probably lose his position. Even against his better conscience, he acquiesced to their cry, "his blood be on us and on our children." He then delivered Jesus to be crucified, having reminded them that they had condemned Jesus to death in their own court for blasphemy, and that he was only carrying out their edicts. **Mt. 27 26**

As we have seen, Pilate had tried to avoid condemning Jesus to death. He tried to move the crowd to pity by scourging Jesus. But this was not the king for whom the Jews were waiting. When Pilate had cried to them "Ecce homo"—"Behold the man!"—they saw only someone with blood on his brow from a thorny crown wearing a purple robe mocking his lack of kingly authority, someone who was weak from scourging and fatigued and pitiful. This moved the crowd against him. They looked for someone who could "deliver Israel"— a victorious leader who could conquer the Romans and bring them longed-for freedom. They were utterly tired of the Roman yoke and weary of generations of captivity as a conquered, enslaved people. They wanted not so much a "Lamb . . . who takes away the sins of the world," as a "Lion of the tribe of Judah" to deliver them by might. They sought not a savior but a deliverer from political servitude. **Jn. 19:5** **Jn. 1:29, RSV** **Rv. 5:5, RSV**

When Pilate had said, "Ecce homo," they had responded "We have no king but Caesar," not out of deep loyalty to Caesar whom many hated for desecrating their temples, but from expediency. Pilate was presenting the one who "thought it not a prize to be called equal with God," but who "emptied himself, taking the form of a servant, . . . and became obedient unto **Jn. 19:15** **Phi. 2:6, literal, 2:7-8, RSV** death, even death on a cross." How could one about to die be their glorious Messiah?

Even Jesus' own disciples were shocked when he allowed his arrest which led to the trial and the cross, and ended at the tomb in seeming defeat. They returned to their fishing nets after his death as if they had been following a hollow dream—a defeated leader.

When Pilate's last effort to free Jesus went awry, the religious leaders and their aids moved among the multitude crying, "Crucify him," and their voices prevailed.

Jn. 19:16, RSV Pilate "handed him over to them to be crucified."

Pilate made sure that a centurion of Rome presided at the execution. Rome alone could carry out the verdict.

Jesus went to his crucifixion followed by a great multitude of the people and of women who did not concur with the verdict and who bewailed and lamented him. But Jesus turning to them said, "Daughters of Jerusalem, weep not for me but for yourselves."

Lk. 23:27, 31

Note 6.

Was Christ Drugged?

"The preaching of the cross is to them that perish foolishness." This was relevant in the first century and it is still a stumbling block to many today, because Christ died for our transgressions. Expect, then, that those who resist Christ as Savior will try desperately to prove that he did not die at all at Calvary.

1 Co. 1:18, KJV

Is. 53:5

One groundless charge is that Jesus did not die on the cross. Instead, his friends bribed the soldiers to give him a drink heavily drugged with a sedative; imbibing it he passed into unconsciousness—was placed in the tomb—came to himself in a few hours—walked out and then went to another location and died at another time.

Let us examine the scriptural and historical evidence that refutes this conclusion. All the Gospels make some contribution to the matter of the drinks.

1. *The first drink.* This was a mock coronation sour wine offered to him in ridicule, imitating the drinks offered to kings about to be crowned. Luke describes the scene: "The rulers were sneering at Him, saying, 'He saved others; let Him save himself, if this is the Christ of God, His Chosen One.' And the soldiers also

Lk. 23:35–38, NAS

91

mocked Him, coming up to Him, offering Him sour wine, and saying, 'If You are the King of the Jews, save Yourself!' " In other words, they joked at his expense. There is no evidence that Jesus took this drink. It is said only that they *offered* it to him. The word translated "sour wine" or "vinegar" (RSV, KJV) is *oxous*, a cheap wine.

2. *The second drink.* This was a strong sedative.

Mk. 15:23
Mt. 27:34

Mark calls it wine mixed with myrrh (Greek, *esmurnis-menon*, from the verb *smurnizō*, meaning to mix with or make like myrrh). Wine (*oinon*) mixed with gall (*cholēs*), says Matthew. Moffatt defines it as "a drink of wine mixed with bitters." Phillips says, "mixed with some bitter drug." It is recorded that this was a strong sedative often mixed by the merciful women of Jerusalem to ease the pain of crucifixion and bring on a merciful stupor. Both Mark and Matthew say plainly that the drink was offered to Jesus, *"but he did not take it"* (*ouk elaben*, Mark), *"he would not drink it"* (Matt.).

Mark's verb translated "offered" is the Greek *edidoun*, in the imperfect tense of incompletion: "they were going to give him" (Wycliffe); "they *tried* to give him" (NAS). The Gospels are clear—he did not receive this second drink; he refused it. After tasting it, he knew what it was; he refused it and endured his suffering for us to the limit.

3. *The third drink.* This again was vinegar or sour wine (*oxous*). Vinegar was often used to moisten the dried, swollen lips of the sufferer so that he could speak plainly—often to make clear his final confession or last words.

Mt. 27:46–48
Jn. 19:29

Jesus had been calling, *"Eli, Eli, lama sabachthani,"* but the words coming through dry lips sounded to the throng as if he were "calling Elijah." Then he called, "I thirst."

"A bowl full of vinegar stood there; so they put a

6. Was Christ Drugged?

sponge full of the vinegar on a hyssop* and held it to his mouth. When Jesus had received the vinegar, he said, 'It is finished'; and he bowed his head and gave up his spirit." Matthew and Mark also say that Jesus received this last drink—vinegar or sour wine. Now he could make his last announcements in a loud clear voice, including his "It is finished," and "Father, into thy hands I commit my spirit."

Jn. 19:29–30, RSV

Mt. 27:48
Mk. 15:35

Jn. 19:30
Lk. 23:46,
KJV

---

*It is suggested that a reed (hyssop) might be too slender to raise a soaked sponge, and that the translator mistook it for the word *hyssopo* which means a spear, lance, or javelin. (See NEB translation—"so they . . . fixed it on a javelin.")

Note 7.

Does a Corpse Bleed?

The Passover season was a sacred one for the Jews. They wanted no crosses decorated by criminals bleeding in agonizing death throes. So the three on the crosses must die in haste and be removed. The military in charge of the crosses, seeing that the two thieves were still alive, broke their legs, thus hastening or insuring death. This was considered a *coup de grâce,* a sort of grace, useful in times of haste.

Jn. 19:31–34, RSV However, as they surveyed the body of Jesus closely, they knew he was "already dead." But they must make technically sure of that, and so they did not break his legs, but they did take a spear and thrust it into his side. No man, of course, could outlive that spearthrust, as Jesus later contended in the presence of doubting Thomas. When one of the soldiers pierced his side with the spear, "there came out blood and water." Here some skeptics claim that Christ was not yet dead, because a corpse doesn't bleed! Let us quote from biblical researcher and historian Jim Bishop: "The Messiah was a dying man and with the physical limitations of man. Most sufferers on the cross did not die from loss of blood. No arteries in wrists or feet had been severed, though there was considerable loss from thorns and wounds. The cause of death in Roman crucifixion was never loss of blood. It was usually asphyxiation. The thieves did not suffer the swift progressive weakness of Jesus, for he had been beaten and given no food and water since the night before—almost fourteen hours. Jesus was closer to death than the robbers. . . . "The man with the spear said this one was dead. He waved them away and stood back a pace. He held his lance midway down the shaft and drew it back aiming for the right side of the chest. He would make certain this one was not feigning death. The spear flipped forward and drove inward between the fifth and sixth rib. It went through the pleura and the thin part of the lung and stopped in the pericardium. The dead do not ordinarily bleed but the right auricle of the human heart holds liquid blood after death and the outer sac holds a serum called hydropericardium. When the soldier withdrew the spear, blood and waterlike serum were seen to emerge and drip down the side of the body."[1]

It was the certain fatality of the Roman spearthrust that Christ used with his "doubting Thomas."

Jn. 20:27, 28

1. Jim Bishop, *The Day Christ Died* (New York: Harper & Bros., 1957).

Note 8.

"It Is Finished"

Christ did not say, "*I* am finished."

He came to earth to be the pattern or image of the Father: He so lived that he could say, "He who has seen me has seen the Father."

Jn. 14:9, RSV

Jn. 17:4, KJV
Mk. 10:45

"I have finished the work which thou gavest me to do," he said in his prayer in Gethsemane. Christ gave his life as a ransom for many. He was paying that ransom with his death. He had become the "Lamb of God," the sufficient sacrifice for the sins of the world. In three days God would put his stamp of approval on this gift by raising him from the dead.

Mt. 20:19
1 Co. 15:3–4

1 Pe. 3:18–19

Ep. 4:8–10

Now would come the finish of the waiting time for souls in Hades—the waiting place of the dead—who had or would now believe in his messiahship and saviorship. They would be transferred to that true Paradise which is at the right hand of God—no longer captive. Finished would be the pains, the tears, the treasons, the trials and the temptations that they and he had known.

1 Co. 15:56, 55

The "sting of death is sin," and death stung him on the cross. As a bee leaves its sting in the wound and dies, so death left its sting in him, and now is powerless to destroy those who trust in him.

He died, as he promised to die. The Father had given

his Son, and the Son had given his life—it was all that they could do. It remains for all to believe in and receive this gift and make it their assurance of eternal life.

When Jesus called out, "Finished," he had finished what he had come to do. Enough blood had been shed and it would be sufficient for the redemption of the whole human race for those who would accept it. Christ could say to the Father, "I have finished." All the works that he came to accomplish in his incarnation were finished at Calvary. Only one question then remained: Would God, by raising his Son from the dead, make authentic and acceptable this "finished" work and life?

In his sermon at Pentecost, the Apostle Peter said, "Jesus of Nazareth, a man attested to you by God with miracles and wonders and signs which God performed through Him in your midst . . . this man, delivered up by the predetermined plan and foreknowledge of God, you nailed to a cross by the hands of godless men and put Him to death. And God raised Him up again, putting an end to the agony of death since it was impossible for Him to be held in its power. For David says . . . "Thou wilt not . . . allow Thy Holy One [Christ] to undergo decay." *Ac. 2:22–27, NAS*

Ps. 16:10

Of David's psalm, Peter said, "David . . . foresaw and spoke of the resurrection of the Christ, that he was not abandoned to Hades, nor did his flesh see corruption. This Jesus God raised up, and of that we are all witnesses." *Ac. 2:29–32, RSV*

Jesus had finished the work God had given him to do in the days of his flesh. Now the Father will finish the work there is for him to do by manifesting his power in raising his Son from the dead on the third day, thus delivering his body from corruption and putting his stamp of approval on the finished work of his Son. *Ro. 4:25; 8:32–35*

Note 9.

Who Sealed and Guarded the Tomb?

Mt. 20:18–20, RSV

After the death of Jesus, the attention of religious and political power centered on the tomb. Jesus had foretold his last days before he lived them: "we are going up to Jerusalem; and the Son of man will be delivered to the chief priests and scribes, and they will condemn him to death, and deliver him to the Gentiles to be mocked and scourged and crucified, and he will be raised on the third day." He had given his resurrection as the proof and imprimatur of God upon his claim to be the Son of God, the true Messiah and King of Israel. Both the Jewish leaders who pressured Pilate to cru-

Mt. 27:62–66, RSV

cify him, and Pilate himself, who at last ordered it, were excited and anxious. Religion was saying to government, "Sir, we remember how that impostor said, while he was still alive, 'After three days I will rise again.' Therefore order the sepulchre to be made secure [sealed] until the third day. . . . Pilate said to them, 'You have a guard of soldiers; go, make it as secure as you can.' So they went and made the sepulchre secure by sealing the stone and setting a guard."

This question arises: Were the guard Pilate's own soldiers or were they part of the temple guard? Pilate said, "You have your guard." There are two Greek words for "guards" or "soldiers." When the governor,

9. Who Sealed and Guarded the Tomb?

Pilate, had Jesus scourged by his own soldiers to move the crowd to pity, the word for soldier is *stratiōtai*. After the resurrection, worried about the empty tomb, the earthquake, the darkness, etc., the chief priests and elders bribed "the soldiers" to say that while they slept on guard the disciples came and stole the body. Here again the word is *stratiōtai*, indicating Pilate's soldiers, some of whom had been at the cross—breaking legs, thrusting spears, and seeing that death was real. Mt. 27:27 Mt. 28:12

The word "guard" is *koustōdias*, which can also mean temple guard, as other translators claim—*The Living Bible*, for instance. One historian states that there were a great many guards in religious employ in Jerusalem and its environs. They guarded the temple and did other service at the behest of the priests and elders. The word *koustōdias* has often indicated "custodians" in the judgment of many translators. Mt. 28:65, RSV

It has been stated that when Pilate was pressed to put his own soldiers on guard at the tomb, he demurred. Some contend that he had too few armed men at his command and had sent to the Syrian prefect nearby asking to borrow some of his military personnel. But the Syrian sent back word to Pilate that he himself had too few soldiers and he feared that Rome was spreading herself too thin and might lose her kingdom around the world if she deployed her forces too lavishly. So Pilate said to the Jewish leaders, "You have your own guard [*koustodia*—watch, guards, custodians], so go your way and make it as sure as *you* can." *The Living Bible* says, "Use your own temple police. They can guard it safely enough." On the other hand, a number of translators imply that Pilate did offer his soldiers to the priests. *The New English Bible* says, "You may have your guard." Moffatt says, "Take a guard of soldiers." Mt. 28:65, NEB, Moffatt

"Some of the guard [*koustodia*] went into the city

99

Mt. 28:11,
NEB, itals
added

Mt. 28:12–
15, NAS

Jn. 20:1–8

Mk. 16:1–4,
RSV

and *reported to the chief priests* everything that had happened." If Pilate had allowed *his* soldiers to guard the tomb, why did they not report all of this to Pilate? What follows signifies that whoever they were, the guards at the tomb were thoroughly convinced that something supernatural had happened that morning because of the earthquake, the darkness, and the empty tomb. This so startled and concerned the religious leaders that "when they had assembled with the elders and counseled together, they gave a large sum of money to the soldiers [*stratiōtai*], and said, 'You are to say, "His disciples came by night and stole Him away while we were asleep." And if this should come to the governor's [Pilate's] ears, we will win him over [persuade him] and keep you out of trouble.' And they took the money and did as they had been instructed; and this story was widely spread among the Jews and is to this day."

The entire concocted story is stupid on the face of it. If the guards—all of them—were asleep, how did they know what happened? The condition of the neatly folded napkin and the orderly clothes once heavy with spices and pitch, unwrapped and left behind but the body gone—none of this spells hurried burglarizing.

What of the punishment for sleeping on watch if they had been Pilate's soldiers? Some authorities claim it would have been crucifixion with head downward— Rome would have been furious. Can one imagine *all* of the guard asleep through all the commotion and the breaking of the seal? What was the "seal"? Some say the tomb was sealed—that is, made safe against pillage —by its immensity. The women coming to the tomb "were saying to one another, 'Who will roll away the stone for us from the door of the tomb?' And looking up, they saw that the stone was rolled back—it was very large." Authorities state that it may have weighed two thousand pounds or more, and had sealed and

9. Who Sealed and Guarded the Tomb?

made safe the tomb by being rolled downward to fit into the stone slot made for it. Slinging it backward and upward again would have taken great strength and probably a lever of some kind. Could this be done silently by a few men? All of the disciples, save John, had fled after the arrest in the garden and were in fear and hiding. It was not they who moved the stone!

Was the "seal" perhaps a cord stretched across the stone and fastened to the rock of the tomb by a lump of clay to guard against any such theft? And woe to anyone removing this seal! Would the whole group of alert guards permit this? Or was it some seal of Rome, as used on a letter, that no one dared remove? Could any of this have escaped the eyes and ears of all the guards? *Or was it the hand of God?*

The guard was terrified enough to be kept from telling the truth only by a "large sum of money"—a substantial bribe. And only a bribe would lead them to tell their outlandish story of the very "theft" they were sent to avoid, promising to try their best to make Pilate believe it and yet feel scarcely to blame! The story is still told and believed by some today who spiritually fight the glorious truth of the bodily resurrection of the Lord.

Mt. 28:15, NAS, TEV, NEB

Let us face it—brazen bribery on the part of the religious leaders had brought about the subtle arrest that led to an unjust trial that led Christ to a cross. It now led to the lie that would try to deny his majestic rising from the dead.

This book does not concentrate on dealing with the resurrection of Christ from the dead. It deals mainly with his trial and death. But let this much be said: from Easter on, the people began to see Christ alive— to touch him, to talk with him, to eat with him, and to walk with him—first the women, then the disciples, then more than five hundred at one time. How many more there were than recorded only God knows.

1 Co. 15:4–7

Note 10.

The Centurion

There is an ancient and persistent legend that the name of the centurion who presided at the crucifixion of Christ and made his confession there was Longinus Francinus. The legend states that when the soldier pierced Christ's side with a spear and saw with astonishment that blood and water flowed out of the wound, some of those drops of blood fell upon his eyes, which had been infected, and immediately cured them.

The history of martyrs tells us that Longinus believed in Christ from that day on and became a monk in Caesarea for twenty-eight years until he was murdered for his faith.

It was further believed that the centurion, who for the last time wet the lips of the dying Christ, together with another centurion named Pretonius, and Pilate's wife, Claudia Procula, were the first Gentiles to accept Christ, which they did on that very day when Jerusalem had cast him out and slain him.

There are some striking things about the death of Jesus. It was planned far ahead. He and the Father had agreed that the Father would give his Son and the Son would give his life a ransom for many, as the Lamb of

Jn. 10:11–18   God. On earth he defined this purpose, "I came to *give* my life." He foretold to his disciples how he would be arrested and condemned to death and die on a cross in Jerusalem. None could deter him, try as Peter did. When Pilate said to Jesus, "Do you not know that I have power to release you, and power to crucify you?" Jesus said, "You would have no power over me unless it had been given you from above." Jesus did not have to die.

Jn. 19:10–11, RSV

He could have escaped and disappeared from that motley crowd on Golgotha as he had escaped those who would have killed him by precipitation over the cliff at Nazareth. He could have gone to the province of Perea to escape the jurisdiction of Pilate and gone free.

Lk. 4:16–29

Did Christ have something definite to do about the *timing* of his death on the cross? As our drama says, people often lingered for forty-eight hours on the cross. Jesus died in four short hours. Victims of crucifixion seldom died from loss of blood or from exhaustion. They usually died of asphyxiation. A total of five times the Gospel writers say that Jesus spoke with a *loud voice* until the very end. Matthew, Mark, and Luke all record his sayings from the cross uttered in this loud voice. This was especially true in his saying, "Eloi, Eloi, lama sabachthani." Then he "cried again with a loud voice and yielded up his spirit," or "gave up the ghost."

Mt. 27:46, 50, RSV, KJV
Mk. 15:34, 37
Lk. 23:46

The centurion is shocked by the suddenness of it all. "When the centurion, who was standing right in front of Him, saw the way He breathed His last, he said, 'Truly this man was the Son of God.'"

Mk. 15:39, NAS

The two thieves evidently had energy left, for the soldiers had to break their legs to hasten their death, but they were surprised to see that Christ was dead already. It was so hard for them to believe this that they made sure of the unbelievable by piercing him with a spear—and out came blood and water, the sign of death.

103

Lk. 23:46,
RSV, itals
added
Mt. 27:50,
KJV, RSV,
itals added

Was this timing voluntary? He said, "Father, into Thy hands I *commit* my spirit." Elsewhere it is recorded that he "*gave* up the ghost"—"yielded up his spirit."

John Masefield in his play *The Trial of Jesus*[1] includes this startling incident in Act III. When Longinus, the centurion, is handing Pilate the report of Christ's crucifixion, Procula, Pilate's wife, beckons to the centurion and begs him to tell her how the prisoner died. After Longinus answers, she suddenly asks: "Do you think he is dead?"

"No, lady, I don't."

"Then where is he?" asks Procula.

"Let loose in the world, lady, where neither Roman nor Jew can stop his truth."

Calvary for many had become not a day of defeat but a day of victory.

---

1. New York: Macmillan, 1925.

Note 11.

The Sign on the Cross

It was customary, historians tell us, in the days of Roman crucifixion, to fasten onto the cross a written sign. The words gave the name of the criminal being executed as well as the crime for which this penalty was being exacted. It is evident that this custom was observed in the crucifixion of Jesus.

Historians with the knowledge of the Roman methods of execution have described the cross in this fashion. The *patibulum*—horizontal beam of the cross —was of considerable weight and often borne separately from the huge upright beam to which it would later be fastened. This piece was so shaped as to be mortised into the upright beam when they came together at the place of crucifixion. Many think that the laborious task of digging the hole for the upright and planting and firming it in the ground was done previously to avoid delay. It was the cross-piece, then, which Christ bore on his shoulders part of the way to the hill of Golgotha, that held the sign telling the meaning of his execution.

While there is a slight difference in the wording of the sign as recorded by the four Gospel writers, let us take the exact title reported to us by John the Apostle, who probably spent more time than any other disciple at that cross. For it is said that others forsook him, that Peter followed "afar off," and that "all his acquaintances stood at a distance" at the crucifixion. We know, however, that John stood close and unhurried enough to converse with his Master about his mother and John's care of her. John writes that the sign read, "Jesus of Nazareth, the King of the Jews."

Some of the Jews complained vehemently about this wording. Why? Was not this one of their accusations against him—that this man "made himself a king"? Pilate of course had proved that he had not but that Jesus had told them to pay tribute to the Roman emperor where tribute was due. Jesus said that his kingdom was a religious not a political one.

Why then did the Jews want Pilate to change the wording to, "He said, I am King of the Jews"? For the Jewish theocracy to accept one as their king meant to accept him as their Messiah, the One who would deliver Israel from her enemies—from Roman domination. To such a person the Jews would owe their highest loyalty; therefore, many used the titles *King* and *Messiah* synonymously. Pilate had already pled with them, "Shall I crucify your King?" But it was unthinkable to them to accept this man as King and Messiah when he had made no step towards doing what their concept of a Messiah called for. They had told Pilate plainly that Jesus had blasphemed in claiming to actually be Messiah and King. This was their death sentence assigned to him: "We have a law, and by that law he ought to die, because he made himself the Son of God." Jesus had made clear that he claimed to be that as well as the Messiah who would come again in his glory with the holy angels to be welcomed and recognized by all.

Pilate and his soldiers had presented him to the multitude clothed in a king's vestment and crown, but the

Mt. 26:56, 58
Mk. 14:54

Lk. 22:54; 23:49
Jn. 19:25–27

Jn. 19:21, RSV

Lk. 1:68–75

Jn. 19:15

Jn. 19:7, RSV

Lk. 22:67–69

106

crowd would not have Jesus, claiming that he was an impostor and a fraud. Thus they asked Pilate to change the sign so it would read that he only *said* he was a king.

Stubbornly, perhaps bravely in a last act of courage, Pilate had insisted in placing on the cross the statement of who this man truly was—their King! In spite of his former cowardice, was Pilate now stating that he was standing by his deepest conviction; that in his opinion this man being crucified was a king, a Messiah, the self-admitted Son of God? At any rate, Pilate would allow no one to change the sign, saying, "What I have written I have written."

Jn. 19:22

"Jesus of Nazareth, the King of the Jews." Pilate chose the wording, and it is difficult to know what was in his heart and mind; but let us name some possibilities.

1. Did it come deep from Pilate's heart and conscience? Jesus had affected him greatly. Three times Pilate sought to release him saying, "I find no fault in him." Was it the more than human stance and character of this man with his fearlessness, his miracles and clear teaching that Pilate saw in Jesus? Was his claim that incredible? Was the sign the outward evidence of a secret conviction that this was more than a man he had permitted to be crucified?

2. Was it a cheap sneer at this arrogant carpenter who had illusions of grandeur and royalty and met the fate of trying to rival Caesar?

3. Was it a jibe to embarrass the Jews? Pilate despised them. Was he saying, "This is the only king of which you slaves are worthy!" when he refused to abate their anger by changing the sign?

The keen Roman historian, Giovanni Papini, wrote, "Pilate was in haste to have that troublesome, innocent man taken away. . . . He wanted to get rid of his own

107

corroding uneasiness so painfully like remorse. Although he had washed and dried his hands, that man in his silence seemed to be sentencing him to a penalty worse than death. . . . To vent on those who caused it, he had dictated the words of the titulus, or superscription, which was fastened above the dead man's head." [1]

The sign was written in three languages: Greek, Latin, Hebrew. Jerusalem was at the crossroads of the world, so all men might read it. Greek was the language of culture and knowledge, Latin the language of law and learning, Hebrew the language of revealed religion. Christ is a universal king of a universal church. Thus even as he was dying, it was so that "on his head were many crowns."

Rv. 19:12,
KJV

The procurator's last edict of dry brevity was the most profound—"I am forced to make you a present of this man's life, but I do not deny what I have said: Jesus is a Nazarene, which also means Saint, and he is your king—I wish all men to know how his enemies treat saints and kings. For this reason I have written the inscription in Latin and Greek as well as Hebrew. Now be off—I have endured you long enough. '*Quode, scripsi, scripsi*' (What I have written, I have written)." [2]

---

1. *The Life of Christ*, translated by Dorothy Fisher (New York: Harcourt, Brace), p. 351.
2. Ibid.

Note 12.

Did Jesus Really Rise from the Dead?

Strange that even in his own apostolic company there should be latent or even active doubts of Christ's rising. One of his disciples frankly expressed doubt some time after the resurrection. Some of the other disciples had borne steady witness that they had seen him in the flesh; they "told what had happened on the road, and how he was known to them in the breaking of bread." Lk. 24:35, RSV
Was it the way in which he broke bread as usual, the way he said the blessing, his customary table manners that made them cry in their hearts, "It is the Lord"?

The difficulty was that Thomas was absenting himself from some of the meetings of the twelve, and when the other disciples said to him, "We have seen the Lord," he still could not believe. "Unless I shall see in His hands the imprint of the nails, and put my finger in the place of the nails, and put my hand into His side, I will not believe." After eight days of waiting Thomas was with them when they met. Jesus, entering the room, said, "Peace be with you." Then, to Thomas, " 'Reach here your finger, and see My hands; and reach here your hand and put it into My side.' [The gash was large enough.] Thomas answered and said to Him, 'My Lord and my God.' " Jn. 20:24–28, NAS

Thomas was the lackey of logic, a slave of the test

109

tube, limited to his animal senses of touch and sight even in matters of faith. For this Jesus rebuked him, "Because you have seen Me, have you believed? Blessed are they who did not see, and yet believed."

Jn. 20:29, NAS

Some, fearing the persistent debt of responsibility that would be theirs if they believed Jesus' claims about himself and their debt and obedience to him, have honestly or viciously, feverishly or defensively, searched eagerly to discover certain discrepancies, contradictions and differences in the accounts and the details and their order, trying thus to destroy the truth that Jesus Christ arose.

Each witness told the resurrection story as he remembered it. Many saw him alive and went out to witness to the fact: Mary Magdalene related how he called her name and she answered, and how she held him to delay him from going back to the Father; two other women saw the stone rolled away; other women passed by the temple guard that had watched the tomb; two other disciples described the empty tomb and the wrapped clothes and the folded napkin; a half dozen more had their supper with him; two more talked with him that evening along an Emmaus Road, a few disciples fishing heard him command them where to fish and were amazed by the full nets that exposed the wisdom of his supernatural knowledge; many answered his call inviting them to "come and have breakfast," and then rushing to him on the shore they broke the fast and ate with him. They all knew it was the Lord. Five hundred saw him alive and well in a short space of time.

Jn. 20:11–18

Mt. 28:1–11

Jn. 20:1–11

Lk. 24:36–43; 13–35
Jn. 21:1–14, RSV

1 Co. 15:6, 7

Had all these witnesses felt they should gather together and match every detail as they saw it to harmonize their stories in every feature, what better reason would the world have needed to say it was all false, manufactured testimony?

12. Did Jesus Really Rise from the Dead?

The faith in their discovery that their Master was alive was vital enough for them to march out to tell the story in farm, hamlet, village, city, temple and synagogue. They compassed land and sea with their vindicated gospel. Thousands would accept the claims of Jesus' proven Lordship and victory.

Each of the writing apostles wrote of the resurrection as he saw it—it was not the borrowed witness of fables and developing myth penned by some aftergenerations. Famous archaeologists William Albright and Sir William Ramsay, and biblical scholar Dr. John A. T. Robinson attest to the Gospels as mid-first-century accounts.

Were the New Testament writers trustworthy? This is basic. One might ask, "Do you believe that Caesar, Cicero, and Washington really lived?" Your answer is "Yes," I suppose. "Have you ever seen them?" Your answer is, "No." "Then how do you know that they once existed?" This answer would have to suffice, "I believe the testimony handed down by those who said they saw these people." The skeptic could retort, "How do you know those who gave testimony were trustworthy?" Your answer had better be established and reasonable. The burden of proof is on the part of the doubter: What reason did witnesses have to lie? Were they willing to pay a price for their testimony?

The apostles who testified orally and in writing concerning the existence of Christ, his character, his word, and his works, were willing to suffer death for this testimony. Note the tremendous suffering and persecutions that Christ's disciples were willing to undergo when they witnessed concerning his words and work. Why should they be willing to pay with their lives for a lie?

Let us name the disciples and study how they died: St. Andrew: Crucified roped to a cross for three days.

Died saying, "Accept me, O Christ Jesus, Whom I saw, Whom I loved, and in Whom I am" (*The Lives and Deaths of the Holy Apostles*, Dorman Newman).

St. Bartholomew: In the history of Abdias, "Bartholomew converted the king, angering the king's brother and the priests who beat and crucified him."

St. James, son of Alphaeus: Was crucified.

St. John: Often persecuted and once threatened with death in boiling oil, but escaped and died a natural death at Ephesus.

St. Mark: He was dragged by rope through the streets of Alexandria until he died (*A History of Eastern Christianity*, Aziz S. Atiya).

St. Philip: Was martyred at age eighty-seven at Hierapolis (*The Lives of the Twelve Apostles*, Dorman Newman).

St. Matthew: The Babylonian Talmud reports him condemned to death by the Sanhedrin.

Ac. 12:1–2 St. James, son of Zebedee: Murdered by King Herod in A.D. 33.

St. Thomas: Pierced to death in Madras, India.

St. Thaddaeus-Jude: Killed with arrows in Persia.

St. James, brother of Jesus: Thrown from the temple and clubbed to death by scribes and Pharisees.

St. Peter: Crucified head down in Rome under Nero.

St. Simon Zelotes: Was slain after preaching Christ in Persia (Dorotheus, Bishop of Tyre in A.D. 300).

Would such as these thus suffer and die for a known falsehood?

Note 13.

The Reliability of Biblical Authorship

A. The Early Date of New Testament Writings

Some critics have suggested that some or all of the Gospels and Epistles were the result of decades or generations of myths, retellings, hazy memories and growing legends; that some of them were written even centuries after the happenings. But writer after writer in the New Testament avers the validity of what he writes:

JOHN: "That . . . which we have heard, which we have seen with our eyes, which we have looked upon and touched with our hands, concerning the word of life . . . we proclaim also to you." "He who saw it has borne witness, and he knows that he tells the truth— that you also may believe."

1 Jn. 1:1–3, RSV

Jn. 19:35, RSV

LUKE: "Inasmuch as many have undertaken to compile a narrative [to give an account] of the things which have been accomplished among us, just as they were delivered to us by those who from the beginning were eyewitnesses [the original eyewitnesses] and ministers of the word, it seemed good to me also, having followed all things closely for some time past [having investigated everything carefully from the beginning, NAS], to write an orderly account."

Lk. 1:1–4, RSV

Sir William Ramsay, with a mind for history and a sharp spade for archaeology, came to the conclusion that "Luke is an historian of the first rank—he should be placed among the greatest of historians."

MARK writes his records of the life and teaching which he had experienced during Christ's day in the flesh. Tradition says that he and Peter continuously cooperated in ordering the facts of the Galilean as they knew him.

2 Pe. 1:16–18, RSV
Cf. Mt. 17:1–8

PETER: "We did not follow cleverly devised myths when we made known to you the power and coming of our Lord Jesus Christ, but we were witnesses of his majesty. . . . We heard this voice borne from heaven, for we were with him on the holy mountain."

MATTHEW: Bishop Polycarp, a disciple of John the Apostle, claimed that "Matthew published his Gospel among the Hebrews in the language of the Jews at a time when Paul and Peter preached and founded a church in Rome." The church fathers Irenaeus in the second century A.D., Origen in the third century, and Eusebius in the fourth century also claim that Matthew composed his Gospel in Hebrew.

Archaeologists of highest rank reiterate their confidence in the biblical manuscripts. As a young man I heard Dr. Melvin Grove Kyle, known as "Mummy" Kyle, defending the Scripture's veracity from his *The Deciding Voice of the Monuments in Biblical Criticism* (1912), say, "The Gospels were written by those who were there. The story is the story of their lives."

The resurrection was witnessed by hundreds who saw Christ alive (see Note 12).

The Gospels were written *within the life time of the writers.*

Form critics should admit that traditions may take generations to develop—even centuries. The disciples

13. The Reliability of Biblical Authorship

were penning their Gospels and letters within their own lifetime. Peter at Pentecost was reviewing these things in his great sermon less than two months after the resurrection! Some three thousand were added to the early church after that sermon. No time here for myths and traditions to have "formed." Many of the people listening could confirm these things because they themselves had seen and heard them. Peter could challenge the doubters with these words, "Men of Israel, hear these words: Jesus of Nazareth, a man attested to you by God with mighty works and wonders and signs which God did through him in your midst, as you yourselves know. . . ." This Jesus was their contemporary. As witnesses for him they had this advantage over us today.

Ac. 2:22, RSV

A host of scholars, archaeologists, historians and critics agree that before myth could become fact, and traditions could become beliefs, the Bible authors were writing their convictions.

William Albright, considered by many to be the world's greatest biblical archaeologist, has written, "We can say emphatically that there is no longer any solid basis for dating any book of the New Testament after 80 A.D." In his *From the Stone Age to Christianity* he continued, "Only modern scholars who lack both the historical method and perspective can spin such a web of speculation as that from which some critics have surrounded the Gospel tradition." John A. T. Robinson, outstanding scholar, in his *Redating the New Testament,* claims that "the whole of the New Testament was written before the Fall of Jerusalem in 70 A.D." [1]

---

1. William F. Albright, *From the Stone Age to Christianity* (New York: Doubleday Archer Books, 1957); John A. T. Robinson, *Redating the New Testament* (Philadelphia: Westminster, 1976).

B. The Trustworthiness of the Writings of John

Though with hesitation, some scholars debate the authority of the Johannine tradition. A host of scholars and believers, however, acclaim it. The latter hold that John, the Apostle and disciple of Christ, under the Spirit's guidance, wrote the Book of Revelation and the Epistles and Gospel that bear his name.

One reason for this belief is the similarity and striking uniformity of John's prologue to the Gospel and the opening statements in the first epistle and Revelation —namely the preexistence of Christ and his eternal character:

Rv. 1:1, 4, 17, RSV

Revelation: "The revelation of Jesus Christ which God gave him [John] to show his servants what must soon take place. . . . John to the seven churches that are in Asia: Grace to you and peace from him who is and *who was* and who is to come, . . . and from Jesus Christ the faithful witness, and the firstborn of the dead, and the ruler of kings on earth. . . . When I saw him, I fell at his feet as though dead. But he laid his right hand upon me, saying 'Fear not, I am the *first* and the last, and the living one.'"

1 Jn. 1:1–2, RSV

John's First Epistle: "That which *was from the beginning,* which we have heard, which we have seen with our eyes, which we have looked upon and touched with our hands, concerning the word of life—the life was made manifest and we saw it . . . the eternal life which *was* with the Father."

Jn. 1:1,14, RSV

John's Gospel: "In the *beginning* was the Word, and the Word was with God, and the Word was God. . . . And the Word was made flesh and dwelt among us, full of grace and truth; we have beheld his glory, glory as of the only Son [the word in Greek means "only begotten," "unique"] from the Father."

Jn. 16:12–13, RSV

Jesus said to his disciples, "I have . . . many things

116

13. The Reliability of Biblical Authorship

to say to you, but you cannot bear them now. When the Holy Spirit of truth comes, he will guide you into all the truth." What follower of Christ was better qualified to be the recipient of such revelations than John? He was dearest to Christ, the disciple "whom Jesus loved"; he sat in the seat of honor next to Christ at important meals; at the greatest crises in Christ's life when he needed the undergirding of masculine friendship, John was there: at the transfiguration and his agony in the garden, John was the one who followed him into the courtyard and heard the trial before the High Priest; he was the only disciple to stand by Jesus at the cross. There Jesus handed over to him the custody of his mother—who later lived near him at home at Ephesus. How often he must have talked with Mary about the innermost thoughts her son must have shared with her. John was the first disciple to discover that the tomb was empty.

Jn. 13:23; 21:20

Lk. 8:51–56; 9:28–30 Mk. 14:32–34 Jn. 18:15–16; 19:25–27

Jn. 20:1–5

John, then, became the great champion of the deity of Christ, although all the Gospel writers declare it. "These [signs] are written that you may believe that Jesus is the Christ, the Son of God."

Jn. 20:30–31, RSV

Jerome, the great fourth-century historian of the disciples and martyrs, stated that John wrote the Gospel at the request of the bishops of Asia to answer the Ebionites who openly asserted that Christ did not live before he was born to Mary—that he was not pre-existent. As his evidence John would use those facts, sayings and works of Christ that were well known to him.

One of the church historians and scholars, Eusebius, relates that while John was at Ephesus, a great leader and presbyter, several of the church leaders and disciples gathered at Ephesus to urge John to write his own Gospel. John demurred but suggested that they fast and pray for three days to see what might be revealed to them, and then tell it to one another. Andrew was the first to certify that it was revealed to him that, "John was to write all things in his own name." The others agreed, as did John, in this conviction.

Another reason for John to write his own Gospel was to add evidence that the other disciples had not included: "When he had read Matthew, Mark, and Luke, he approved indeed the substance and declared that the things they wrote were true, but some had given the history of only one year"—the year that followed the imprisonment of John, and in which John the Baptist was put to death. So John, passing this year and some events already put forth, related the events of the earlier period before John was imprisoned, "so that it should be manifest to those who shall diligently read the volumes of the four evangelists."

When sent into exile on the Isle of Patmos, John wrote the Apocalypse (Revelation). After Domitian, the imprisoning emperor, was stabbed to death by Stephanus, the Senate, despising Domitian's brutality, commuted John's sentence and released him. He went to live in Ephesus. There he dwelt during his old age, wrote his Gospel, encouraged the churches and as Jerome and others contend, died peacefully about A.D. 100.[1]

1. *Encyclopaedia Britannica*, 1942, vol. 13.

Part Three
CHRISTIANS AND JEWS

Christians' and Jews' Attitudes toward Each Other

It is of vital importance for the spiritual, social and economic health of the world that Christians and Jews have the right attitudes toward each other. Malfunctions in this area have brought to history untold pain, agony, death and misunderstanding. God-guided attitudes can bring love, healing, peace and understanding. What are some of the attitudes that Christians should embrace toward the Jews?

A. Gratitude and Thanksgiving

In the first place, Christians should be eternally grateful to the Jews. We have many reasons to be.

1. *For the Ten Commandments.* These ten fundamentals of enduring morality came to us through the Jewish leader, Moses, straight from the heart and hand of God. As basic to life as the scale is to harmonious musical composition, so these God-given secrets of beneficial thought and behavior are the norm for and solution to our moral problems. These were passed on to us and the nations to follow.

2. *For the Old Testament Prophets* and their God-given precepts, persuasions, prophecy and courage, wisdom and warning—both moral and Messianic.

Jn. 14:6

3. *For the Jews who wrote most of the New Testament* after finding Christ as their Messiah, "the way, the truth, and the life." For Matthew, Mark, John, Peter, James, and Paul. The New Testament books were not the results of centuries of growing myths and developing traditions, but were written in the authors' own time about the things "that . . . we have seen and heard," and which "our hands have handled, of the Word of Life."

1 Jn. 1:3, 1,
KJV

4. *For those Christian-Jewish missionaries* who were the first to compass land and sea with the Gospel, sometimes at the cost of their lives.

5. *For the founding of the early churches,* and for the many who were deacons, elders, pastors, and bishops. The Christians found not only their most violent enemies among the Jews, but also their most loyal friends and vital comrades in the faith—they became, as Peter said, "lively stones" in the temple of Christ.

1 Pe. 2:5,
KJV

B. Fairness in Our Attitudes

Admittedly, according to the Gospel records, some of the Jews of Jesus' time were instrumental and influential in bringing about his death by the sentence passed by the Sanhedrin—"he should die because he made himself the Son of God"—and by the pressure put on Pilate to crucify him because "he made himself the King of the Jews." However, we must remember Christ's priestly prayer. In this prayer, he heartily thanked the Father for those of his countrymen who believed on him and were with him "from the beginning" to the end, and for the women who wept for him and gave him of their substance and their hearthsides.

Jn. 17:6, 9,
12, 25

We must not be guilty of making the mistake of holding present-day Jewry responsible for the events

of two thousand years ago. This is as unjust as hating
all Englishmen because during the Revolutionary War
they not only hanged Nathan Hale but refused his request for a Bible and a minister. Anti-Semitism is as
senseless as blaming all Italians of today because Nero
put Rome to the torch and slaughtered the Christians
in the Arena. My father and I do not accept the blame
for our Welsh Druid ancestors who made human sacrifices. Let us all be judged by our words and actions in
the *now*.

C. Understanding the New Covenant of God's Redemption

The great difficulty and challenge to agreement of
mind and heart with God, with humanity, with Jew,
with Christian is the need to understand God's new
covenant—his new plan of redemption which effec-
tively brought to an end the old covenant and plan.
Whether we face these questions alone or in a group,
let it be with a studious, patient and open mind. Let
the Scripture sketch the plans:

1. *First plan and covenant—by sacrifices.* Offerings
and sacrifices were the first means God instituted of
obtaining forgiveness. With repentant hearts, people
brought their offerings of fruit, crops, livestock, etc. to   Ge. 22:13
God.

2. *The temple sacrifices.* For the Jews, sacrifices became centered in the temple in Jerusalem. Hebrews 9
describes the early temple rites. Though worship was   Le. 7
not confined to altars or "temples made with hands,"
there were special privileges in meeting God in the
temple—"The Holy One of Israel in the midst of thee."   Ho. 6:4–6
3. *The inadequacy of this plan.* In the very ritual   Is. 12:8, KJV
and symbolism of the temple worship, says the author   Hb. 9:1–10,
of Hebrews, "The Holy Spirit indicates that the way to   RSV

the sanctuary is not yet opened as long as the outer tent [tabernacle] is still standing (which is symbolic for the present age)." The Old Testament prophets saw later that the people were bringing, not their best, but their poorest to God: the mildewed meal, the sickest sheep, the poorest and the lame cattle. Their heart was not in their worship, and the later temple fell into disrepair. In Samaria, a golden calf became their center of worship. The prophets rebuked them, wooed them and pled with them, but to so little effect that many prophets were stoned and/or killed.

Hb. 10:4–10, RSV

4. *The new plan.* In Hebrews 10 there is a conversation between Christ and the Father. The Son who was in the beginning with the Father says, "It is impossible that the blood of bulls and goats should take away sins. Consequently when Christ came into the world, he said, 'Sacrifices and offerings thou hast not desired, but a body hast thou prepared for me; in burnt offerings and sin offerings thou hast taken no pleasure. Then I said, "Lo, I have come to do thy will, O God." ' "

Hb. 9:11–12, RSV

Christ "appeared as a high priest of the good things that have come. . . . he entered once for all into that Holy Place, taking not the blood of goats and calves but his own blood, thus securing an [our] eternal re-

Hb. 10:9–10, RSV

demption." "He abolishes the first [covenant involving sacrifices] in order to establish the second [the doing of God's will making the first obsolete]. And by that will we are sanctified through the offering of the body of Christ once and for all."

5. *Jewish prophets knew of this plan.* Hundreds of years before the coming of Christ to earth, the prophet

Is. 7:13–14, RSV

foretold it. "O House of David . . . the Lord himself will give you a sign. Behold a young woman [a virgin, KJV] shall conceive and bear a son and shall call his name Immanuel [God is with us]." Now in the same prophecy of Isaiah note the thrilling, minute details of

Is. 53

Christ's characteristics and what will happen to him.

6. *Then he came in the flesh,* in the Incarnation (Latin *en*—in, *karnos*—flesh). Read the story in Matthew 1:18 ff. and Mark 1:1–3, 9–15; 2:1–43 and in Luke 2.

7. *Christ displaces the Passover of the old covenant with the Lord's Supper of the new covenant.* "He took a cup, and when he had given thanks he gave it to them, saying, 'This is my blood of the covenant [Testament] which is poured out for many for the forgiveness of sins. I tell you I shall not drink again of this fruit of the vine until that day when I drink it new with you in my Father's kingdom.'"

Mt. 26:26–29, RSV

The Passover was a political celebration of Israel's deliverance as a people and a nation, remembering the time when the blood of a lamb was smeared on the door lintels so the Israelites and their firstborn were spared from death while the babes of the Egyptians were not. Christ could join this celebration of the deliverance of the Jews, as can we Christians, even as other nations can join our celebration from British bondage in our Fourth of July celebration.

Ex. 12:12–31

In our Passover, the Lord's Supper, the Lamb spiritually frees us from the bondage of sin. It is when the Passover takes over this atonement idea of spiritual deliverance from the guilt and bondage of sin that the difficulty arises with some. In Christ's death the symbols of the Passover and the sacrifices are combined. Christ the one High Priest, having paid the price of man's salvation, would see God approve of his saviorship by raising him from the dead on the third day. Priests never ceased making their animal sacrifices for sin. They could not stop—there were no seats in the temple. Jesus made his one sacrifice of himself for us on the cross, and as our high priest "sat down." There is no further need of sacrifice for sin. Man but needs to accept Christ's.

Hb. 10:7–13

D. Christ Foresaw This Partial Rejection

Jn. 16:1–6
Mt. 5:10–
12; 20:17–
19; 21:23–
45
1 Co. 11:24–
26, RSV

Before he went to Calvary, Christ himself foresaw that he would be rejected as the true Lamb of God by whom we should be delivered. But Jesus at the Passover Feast with his disciples at his "last supper" made himself the Passover Lamb. He said " 'This cup is the new covenant in my blood. Do this, as often as you drink it, in remembrance of me.' For as often as you eat this bread and drink the cup, you proclaim the Lord's death until he comes." For those who believe on him, this feast shall never end for he promised that he would eat and drink with us in his Father's kingdom.

Mt. 26:26–
29

E. The Feast of Tabernacles

Let us remind the Jews that Christ did not seek to destroy their religion but rather to help them fulfill it.

Lv. 23:33–
44

One of the festivals dear to the Hebrew heart was the Feast of Tabernacles. It was a great celebration of Thanksgiving for a plentiful harvest and the ingathering of the fruit. John describes Jesus' visit to Jerusalem

Jn. 7:2–13

for a feast of tabernacles. Jesus' brothers wanted him to go up for the beginning of the feast, which also involved the "pouring of the water," but Jesus had his

Jn. 7:8, RSV

reasons for delaying his visit, saying, "My time has not yet fully come." He stayed in Galilee until the middle of the feast. There was a daily sacrifice.

The feast was usually seven or eight days in duration. The "pouring of the water" took place daily in this way. About the time of the sacrifice the High Priest would take a golden vessel, probably a pitcher, and carry it down empty to the Pool of Siloam, dip it in and mix it with the wine of the sacrifice. Then he would march back amid the blowing of trumpets and

126

expressions of great joy, and pour it out beside the altar from where it flowed down to the valley of Kidron. A choir would sing songs from the prophecy of Isaiah concerning the Jews' salvation. The priests did this for six or seven days.

The "Great Day" of the feast was the last day, and it differed from the others in one significant detail. On this day the High Priest did not dip the pitcher in the pool but carried it back to the altar dry and empty— as though waiting for a more satisfying day and savior. Hard days were ahead and their true Messiah had not yet come. It was for this last day that Jesus had waited and his reason was now evident. The pitcher would be empty until the true Messiah came to deliver the Jews and quench their deeper thirst. Jesus stood in their path as they passed with the empty pitcher and said, "If any one thirst, let him come to me and drink. He who believes in me, as the scripture has said, 'Out of his heart shall flow rivers of living water.'" He meant that the Holy Spirit would make it possible for them to quench their inner thirst with this living water when he was glorified in their hearts and minds. But some did not accept, "so there was a division among the people because of him," as there still is today. Only some say, "This is the Christ."

Christ offered himself to the Jews as the living water, not in anger but in loving concern—as he offered himself as the Messiah to the Samaritan woman at the well, promising her the end of her inner thirst.

So often we hear a rejection of God as being angry or disinterested. How little the world knows of the comfort of a *personal* God who is actually with us, caring and knowing and ready to help.

Through the Bible we can trace the Old Testament promises through to the New Testament fulfillments and bridge the gap between Judaism and Christianity

Jn. 7:37

Jn. 7:37–39, RSV

Jn. 7:43, RSV

Jn. 4:11–15

127

until our faiths become a single tapestry held together by the unbreakable threads of God's love, forgiveness, and renewal.

This verse by Horatius Bonar expresses what our voice of concern and personal witness should be to our Jewish friends:

> I heard the voice of Jesus say,
>   "Behold I freely give
> The living water, thirsty one
>   Stoop down and drink and live."
> I came to Jesus and I drank
>   Of that life-giving stream;
> My thirst was quenched, my soul revived,
>   And now I live in Him.